T0155645

Human-Computer Interaction in Game Development with Python

Design and Develop a Game Interface Using HCI Technologies and Techniques

Joseph Thachil George
Meghna Joseph George

Apress®

Human-Computer Interaction in Game Development with Python: Design and Develop a Game Interface Using HCI Technologies and Techniques

Joseph Thachil George
Hannover, Germany

Meghna Joseph George
Hannover, Germany

ISBN-13 (pbk): 978-1-4842-8181-9
https://doi.org/10.1007/978-1-4842-8182-6

ISBN-13 (electronic): 978-1-4842-8182-6

Managing Director, Apress Media LLC: Welmoed Spahr
Acquisitions Editor: Spandana Chatterjee
Development Editor: James Markham
Coordinating Editor: Mark Powers
Copy Editor: Kezia Endsley

Cover designed by eStudioCalamar

Cover image by Jose Gil on Unsplash (www.unsplash.com)

Distributed to the book trade worldwide by Apress Media, LLC, 1 New York Plaza, New York, NY 10004, U.S.A. Phone 1-800-SPRINGER, fax (201) 348-4505, e-mail orders-ny@springer-sbm.com, or visit www.springeronline.com. Apress Media, LLC is a California LLC and the sole member (owner) is Springer Science + Business Media Finance Inc (SSBM Finance Inc). SSBM Finance Inc is a **Delaware** corporation.

For information on translations, please e-mail booktranslations@springernature.com; for reprint, paperback, or audio rights, please e-mail bookpermissions@springernature.com.

Apress titles may be purchased in bulk for academic, corporate, or promotional use. eBook versions and licenses are also available for most titles. For more information, reference our Print and eBook Bulk Sales web page at http://www.apress.com/bulk-sales.

Any source code or other supplementary material referenced by the author in this book is available to readers on GitHub (https://github.com/Apress). For more detailed information, please visit http://www.apress.com/source-code.

Printed on acid-free paper

Table of Contents

TABLE OF CONTENTS

About the Authors

Joseph Thachil George is an IT security engineer based in Germany. He also worked as a technical consultant for International Game Technology (IGT) in Italy. Joseph is currently pursuing his PhD in computer science and engineering at the University of Lisbon, Portugal. He has an MS in cybersecurity from the University of Florence, Italy. He is also part of the DISIA research group at the University of Florence, Italy, and the research group (INESC-ID Lisbon) at the University of Lisbon, Portugal. His research interests cover automatic exploit generation, exploitation of vulnerabilities, chaining of vulnerabilities, security of web applications, and JavaScript code exploits. At IGT, he has been a part of various projects related to game configuration and integration in various platforms, specializing in Java and Spring Boot–based projects. He has also worked for various companies in India, Angola, Portugal, and the UK and has seven years of experience with various IT companies.

Meghna Joseph George is a cloud engineer based in Germany. She is an AWS-certified solutions architect. She has a BS in system management and an MS in economics.

About the Technical Reviewer

 **Deepak Jadhav** is a game developer based in Bonn, Germany. He received a B.S. in computer technology and an M.S. in game programming and project management. Deepak has been involved in developing games on multiple platforms, including mobiles, consoles, and PCs. He has a strong background in C# and C++, as well as years of experience using Unity, Unreal Engine for Game Development, augmented reality, mixed reality, and virtual reality.

Introduction

The goal of this book is to boost your knowledge of human-computer interaction (HCI) in the context of game production. In computer games, interface design and development are critical. This book focuses on and investigates human-computer interaction (HCI) design in computer game interfaces in order to meet their collaborative and interactive requirements.

We begin with a brief overview of HCI's essential concepts and methods. Following that, we go into the fundamental concepts of gaming interface design and technology. We also look at how to create a gaming interface that is effective in terms of HCI, all using practical Python examples.

We go through the primary concerns game developers and publishers, as well as how various HCI approaches can help tackle these problems. Additionally, we consider "playability" throughout the entire game development process.

Gamification has a strong impact on human-computer interaction based research these days, and we discuss gamification and its applications, as well as how it improves human-computer interaction.

Human-Computer Interaction Research Topics

This book also covers a wide range of research subjects relating to game development based on human-computer interaction with a focus on the theory, apps, practice, and verification in the field of human-computer interaction, with the goal of changing behavior. This approach covers the traditional arenas, including cognition, cognitive science, instructional technology, video games, game-based rehabilitative services, neuro feedback, wellness, universal health care, physical and mental health, machine intelligence, digital technology, and so on. From these perspectives, new scientific approaches, including test results and real-world applications, are strongly encouraged.

Source Code

All source code used in this book can be downloaded from `github.com/apress/hci-gamedev-python`.

CHAPTER 1

Human-Computer Interaction Tools and Methodologies

The core concepts of human-computer interaction (HCI) and its tools and methodologies are presented in this introductory chapter. We will also explore how a computer's interaction with a user/player is meant to provide them with a unique new POV that allows them to connect with the computer. We cover usability, interface patterns, and design for user-computer interactions. Understanding these technologies is crucial to creating effective games and web applications that utilize human-computer interaction.

Fundamentals of Human-Computer Interaction

HCI's main objective is to improve user-computer interactions by making computers more responsive to the game player's input. This is done through the following three interfaces: the command line, the graphical user interface, and a standardized user interface.

© Joseph Thachil George, Meghna Joseph George 2022
J. T. George and M. J. George, *Human-Computer Interaction in Game Development with Python*, https://doi.org/10.1007/978-1-4842-8182-6_1

Advantages of the command-line interface include:

- Use of "options" allows for flexibility.

- Easier for "skilled" players since operations can be accessed rapidly.

- Most efficiently uses the operating system.

Advantages of the Graphical User Interface (GUI) include:

- Uses panels, icons, menu, and arrows that may be moved about with a cursor.

- The best UI for unskilled or new players. However, web applications/games consume a lot of computer resources. Most common interface applications/games have a similar functionality.

Advantages of the standardized user/player interface include:

- Increases training velocity.

- Increases trust from beginner players.

- Expanded range of tasks to be solved by players.

- Expanded choice of applications for the ordinary computer game player.

- Are easy to use.

To better understand what human-computer interaction and usability are, let's take a look at Norman's Model[1], which identifies the main phases of user interaction. This model provides a valid, if simplified, logical framework for design and evaluation. There are seven possible steps to describe human-computer interaction:

---

[1] Norman D.: *The Design of Everyday Things*. Basic Books, 1998.

1.   Formulate the goal.

2.   Formulate the intention.

3.   Identify the action.

4.   Perform the action.

5.   Perceive the status of the system.

6.   Interpret the system's status.

7.   Evaluate the result against the goal.

Norman places the seven phases in the context of the cycle of an interaction and identifies the "execution" (the difference between the user intentions in terms of actions to be carried out and the actions permitted by the system) and the "evaluation" (the difference between the representations provided by the system and what it expects from the user).

In interfaces with poor usability, where the tasks to be done are badly supported, these two evaluations can be useful for identifying discrepancies between what the users would like to do and what they can do (execution) and between what the system presents and what the users do (evaluation). See Figure 1-1. In both cases, it is possible to identify the cognitive distance indicated by the quantity and quality of the information processed by the users in order to bridge the gap.

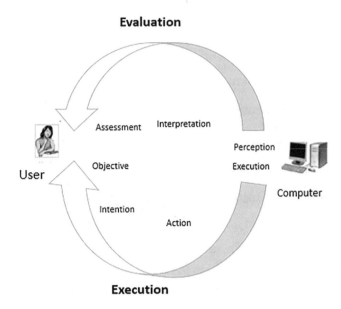

Figure 1-1. *Norman's cycle of interaction*

To better understand these concepts, let's look at various examples.

Digging Deeper

A fairly intuitive example is a game that consists of the numbers 1 to 9, which are all initially available to each of the two players. The players play one at a time. During each turn, the players choose one of the remaining numbers (making it unavailable). If a player has three numbers whose sum is 15, they win.

First you need to understand the problem. Both players share a common goal, which is to win the game. There is also another objective: "If at a certain point I can't win, then I want to prevent the other player from winning". One possible strategy is to choose a number from the remaining numbers that might prevent the other player from winning.

So the "background" activity is remembering the numbers that you already chose, remembering the remaining numbers (and those taken by your opponent), and remembering whose turn it is. This game becomes non-trivial. Suppose you need to design a user interface that makes it easier to play this game. One solution is represented by the interface shown in Figure 1-2.

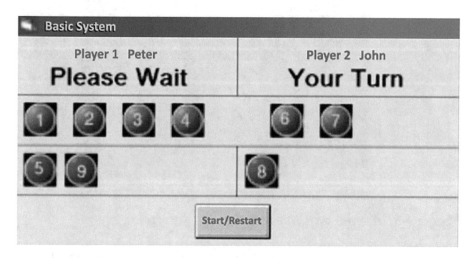

Figure 1-2. *Interface for the game that consists of a choice between numbers to add up to 15*

As you can see, it is clearly highlighted who has to play. It also shows which numbers have been selected (in red) and which are available (in green), as well as who has selected them. However, players still have to understand which number to choose to prevent their opponent from winning. There is a considerable cognitive distance between choosing suitable actions and the user's initial objective. An interface that limits this cognitive load, and so is more usable, is shown in Figure 1-3.

The idea is that the players use a substantially different interface: A 3×3 matrix where one player can place Xs and the other Os. Assuming that the matrix corresponds to numbering, as that indicated by the small matrix on the left, the game becomes like the Tic Tac Toe (known in Italy as Three of a Kind), whereby the aim of the players is to place three elements in a row or diagonally. Understanding if your opponent is about to win now becomes very intuitive, detectable at a glance, and doesn't require particularly complicated processing.

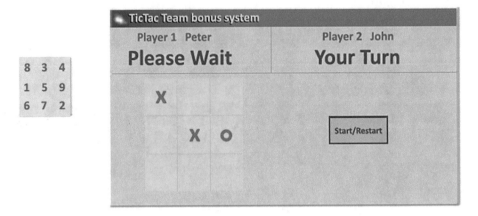

Figure 1-3. *A more intuitive interface for the game*

A fundamental principle of HCI is understanding your users and the tasks they intend to perform. These tasks are the activities necessary to achieve a goal, where the goal can be modifying the status of an application (for example, adding new data) or accessing information contained in applications.

The user interface must allow users to carry out these activities in the most immediate and intuitive way possible. To this purpose, an important phase in the design is the analysis of the tasks, which aims to identify the most relevant tasks and their characteristics.

To understand this, it is important to involve the end users in the design and keep in mind how they currently carry out such activities. This can be accomplished through interviews, workshops, questionnaires, and by observing the users in the usual context. Analyzing tasks can be done at different levels of granularity, also depending on the objectives. It can focus on a person interacting with an application via a computer or it can extend to the whole process and involve several people. The interface design aids in your understanding of the system and its goals.

Designing the Interface

Interface design is about communication with the end users. It's about designing forms and spaces in the context of one specific task or problem[3]. To this purpose, you must avoid considering internal functional aspects alone and find solutions that have a general foundation. Don't rely only on the designer's intuition; instead, you must find the right balance between method and intuition.

The aim is to define clear, economical, convincing solutions that you can operate immediately and that can be more easily assimilated, understood, and remembered. They should immediately attract the users to the important aspects and allow them to reach their goals without errors. Often the simplest solutions are the most usable. Think about sites that, when accessed, start animations that don't provide particular additional information, but are simply tinsel.

Think of the user who perhaps logs in via a slow modem connection and is having to undergo an animation, perhaps without the possibility to skip it, for many minutes.

This does not mean that animation should never be used, but, when it fits, it has to provide something additional and not to be an element for its own sake. For example, animation can be useful for understanding dynamic phenomena that evolve over time. Hence, effective design should reduce the elements to their essence.

One example is the horizontal bar at the top the window that contains applications in Windows PC environments and others: think about how many tasks it can support! This area indicates the name of the file associated with the application, the type of application, if the window is the one currently selected, the ability to minimize or maximize the size of the window, the ability to close it, and the ability to move it around the screen. All thanks to a small rectangular strip, which is also extremely unobtrusive!

Another important aspect in designing user interfaces is how to structure and organize their presentation. To this purpose, there are a series of communication techniques that aim to help the users scroll through the interface, interpret the elements, and find what they are looking for.

What the designer must try to do is to group elements, create hierarchies, represent relationships, indicate order between the elements and, in the end, find an overall balance. Grouping elements is useful for indicating those that are more semantically connected, creating hierarchies serves to highlight the most important elements (for example, those that are accessed most frequently), relationships are used to make users understand how one or more elements can influence other elements and, finally, there can be various types of logical or temporal ordering between groups of elements.

See for example the web page of a popular newspaper in Figure 1-4 to understand how these techniques can be used. As you can see, there is a clear hierarchy between the various elements. The information deemed most important is highlighted in the center with a large image and a title with large fonts. The next most important information is underneath and uses less space, a smaller image, and a smaller font. On the sides there are groupings of information of similar types, such as the services of Repubblica.it and 24 hours (which contain the latest news).

Figure 1-4. *Example of design techniques applied to a web interface*

At the top, there is an example element (Site Search), which is in relation to others. If it's selected, it changes the page to allow users to search the information on the site. Also in the upper area, there is the ability to select a set of elements associated with various sections that are logically ordered between them (politics, news, economics, etc.). You can see, therefore, how all the various relationships are highlighted with design techniques so users can perceive them in the most immediate way.

In general, there are various ways to consider an interactive system. One way is to consider the tasks to be performed to achieve the user's goals and the logical objects needed. This is a logical view of the system that can be discussed with other people involved in the design (end users, clients, interface designers, and software developers). There is another view, which is also logical but is more focused on the interface, and that is to consider the presentations and the interactions and how to move from one presentation to the other. Interactions are identified based on their semantics (the results they allow you to obtain). For example, it can be said that at a certain point you need a selection without specifying the type of mode required to make it (which can be, for example, graphical, vocal, or through a gesture)

There is, then, a possible more concrete description where the methods and techniques of interaction are specified. For example, it can be said that, in a graphical desktop system, selections are made via a list with a scroll bar.

Finally, there is the implementation, which can be in HTML, Java, etc. When designing the interface, the level of abstraction of the starting point can change depending on the case. Sometimes, the tasks to be supported are identified, so those are the starting point and, through subsequent refinements, lead to the implementation. In other cases, you start from an existing implementation and try to understand if indeed it is the best way to support the user's activities. Because of the abundance of information technology, interactive systems may be used in a variety of ways. These ways can be utilized with the help of adaption and interface techniques.

Adaption and Interfaces

The wealth of information technology allows for many uses of interactive systems. User interfaces often have to know how to adapt to the context, which can be considered from three points of view: those relating to the user, the device, and the surrounding environment. As for the user, important aspects are the objectives and related tasks, preferences, and the level of knowledge of the application domain and the methods of interaction.

Regarding the device used for the interaction, it is important to consider the supported modes, the amplitude and the screen resolution, the capabilities, and the connection speed with other devices. Finally, the environment has various aspects that can affect the interaction modes, such as the level of noise and light, and objects that are available. User interfaces have to adapt to these factors for better usability.

There are two types of adaptation. *Adaptability* can be the ability to change aspects at the explicit request of the *user* in accordance with predefined options, or it can be the ability of the *system* to dynamically modify aspects without explicit user requests. While adaptability essentially allows you to choose the methods of interaction with an application from a predefined set, it implies that systems dynamically change with respect to the context.

On the one hand, this implies greater flexibility, but on the other hand, it means that new usability issues can arise if these changes occur in a way that are not easily understood by the users. There are three types of aspects that can be adapted: presentations (layouts, attributes, graphs, etc.), dynamic behavior (navigation methods, enabling and disabling the techniques of interaction, etc.), and the content of the information provided. Figure 1-5 shows an example of an adaptable interface. Depending on the type of user that's visiting, different ways of accessing the application are activated.

Figure 1-5. *Sample adaptable interfaces*

In the case of tourists, the possibilities of accessing information are generic and they see a map of the city and the museum. They can then select items of interest for which they will receive information. In the case of students, the site assumes some basic knowledge, so they can activate lists of elements on the aspects of greater interest. It also shows an interface for an expert, who can compose detailed requests.

Always in the same area, it is possible see an example of interaction that adapts to the device and the environment. In this case, the site considers the users inside a museum and uses a handheld guide to aid their visit (see Figure 1-6). The guide tries to be as unobtrusive as possible, providing a lot of information in a vocal way, to allow the users to appreciate the objects that are in the museum while providing additional information. The visual channel is used by the handheld guide to provide useful information to understand where you are and what other elements of interest are nearby. It also checks the parameters of the guide to access videos that provide information about related topics that are not in the museum.

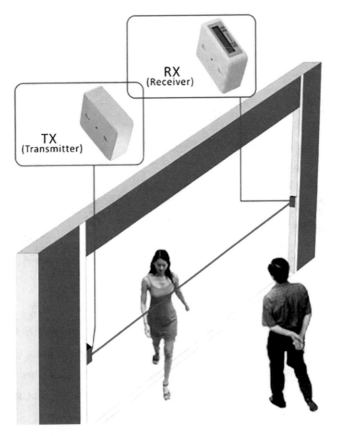

Figure 1-6. Handhelds are used as a support for visiting museums. The visitor's position is detected with infrared devices

This solution was adopted by the Carrara Marble Museum[2] and it depends on the user's location, which is automatically detected. This is achieved through infrared devices on the ceiling at the entrance to each room. They emit a signal that contains a room identifier (see Figure 1-6).

In fact, each device is composed of multiple infrared signal emitters to increase the ease of detection. When the device detects the signal, it identifies the room and automatically emits sound feedback. It shows on the screen where the user is, after which the first selection shows the map of the new room with icons for each work of art.[2]

There are icons for each type and, by selecting an icon, the user receives additional information in a vocal way and can access videos on related topics (if any). This solution is made possible due to the availability of 1GB handhelds that record rich multimedia information.

This limits the interaction with the outside world to detect signals that allow the museum to identify the environment the user is in. Another possible solution would have been to identify the nearest work of art and automatically activate a corresponding voice comment. The limitation of this solution is that it can, in some cases, become too intrusive and provide unwanted comments. Sometimes you need to use multiple devices for such interfaces.

As an example, you can see how an app's UI varies depending on whether it's in landscape or portrait mode. First of all, you need to open the Settings app. Go to Accessibility ➤ AssistiveTouch. Make sure the toggle at the top of the screen is in the On position. Tap one of the four options (Single Tap, Double Tap, Long Press, or 3D Touch) and set it to Open Menu (https://support.apple.com/en-ca/HT202658).

Interfaces of Multi-Device

One of the main issues currently impacting user interfaces is the continuous introduction of new types of interactive devices: from interactive digital wall-mounted telephones to PDAs, telephones UMTS,

---

[2] Ciavarella C., Paternò F.: The design of a handheld, location-aware guide for indoor environments. Personal and Ubiquitous Computing, Vol. 8, n. 2, p. 82-81, Sprinter Verlag, May 2004.

and tablet PCs, to name a few. Interacting with interactive services becomes a multi-device experience. It is important to understand the new issues that are introduced into this context. The first thing to understand is that it isn't possible to do everything through all devices.

There are features of the devices that can make them suitable to support tasks but are inadequate for others. For example, most users would never use (let alone pay for) a service that allows them to use a telephone to watch a movie or a whole game of football, as the experience would be somewhat cramped and would not allow them to appreciate detail. Conversely, if you were stuck in traffic and wanted to find an alternative route, a mobile device is key. In other cases, supported activities can be accessed across different devices, but the modes change.

For example, a hotel booking made via mobile phones with web or WAP access enables users to communicate arrival and departure dates. Using a desktop system, you can comfortably provide an evening of additional information, for example, to express your preferences in terms of rooms, meals, etc. Or the desktop system can present extensive booking forms where various fields can be filled in for different orders, while the mobile site can impose some sequence in providing the request parameters due to the smaller screen.

There are activities through one type of device that can enable or disable activities through another. For example, you can make an airline reservation via a desktop system, and then you can access real-time information via your mobile phone related to the flight you booked. There are also activities that remain the same regardless of the device. For example, logging in remains more or less the same across different types of devices. In adapting to the type of device, it is also necessary to consider the supported modes, because this influences the possibilities of interaction.

Tasks can be influenced by the interaction mode: a set of inputs can require separate interactions through a graphic device, while such information can be provided through a single interaction using a voice interface. There are inherent differences between the various modes.

For example, voice channels are best suited for short messages, to report events and immediate actions, to avoid visual overload, and when users are on the move. The visual channel is more useful for complex or long messages, for identifying spatial relationships, and when actions need to be performed in multiple, noisy environments or when users are stationary.

When a system supports multiple modes (for example, graphical and vocal interaction), the possible implementation techniques is wide. You must consider different ways to combine the modalities: complementary (both modalities are used synergistically to complement interaction), assignment (a specific method is used to create a certain purpose), redundancy (multiple modes are used to achieve the same effect), and equivalence (users choose between multiple modes to achieve the same effect).

This has been an introduction to the fascinating world of the human-computer interaction, explaining its objectives and fundamental concepts and showing application examples. It has witnessed a real explosion of interest and has substantially evolved.

Evolutionary Trends

This evolution continues, driven by the evolution of interaction technologies and the constantly changing user requirements. The continued introduction of new interactive computer devices in our homes, offices, cars, and places of commerce and tourism implies the need to plan a pervasive usability that can guarantee satisfaction in the different contexts of use. This opens up the possibility of creating migration services in the future—interactive services that follow users in their movements and adapt to the new devices available in these new environments. The goal is to allow users to continue the interaction where they left off with the device in the previous environment.

Consider a person who is registering for a service through the system desktop. They suddenly realize that they are late and so take their PDA and continue the registration as they exit the office. When they get into the car, they complete the registration using a voice interaction system, all without having to redo any transactions carried out through previously used devices. The interfaces adapt to the new devices used. This level of multimodality will increase significantly for many reasons.

Some technologies are substantially improving, like those related to voice interaction. They show a growing ability to interpret human input and so have begun to be supported, in a stable way, for interaction via the web. Technologies that detect user presence are diversifying and improving. The improvement of shape recognition techniques and elements in the images is increasing the possibility of interaction through gestures, whereby different functions are activated depending on the recognized gesture. These and other possibilities have the aim of making the interaction with computers similar to that between human beings. This can lead to the affirmation of the paradigm of natural interaction, which guarantees usability that's extremely immediate and spontaneous.

Evaluation of Usability

The usability assessment can be carried out for different purposes. There may be precise goals, such as wanting users to be able to perform a task with a certain number of interactions or in a certain period of time.

There are various methods that are considered when evaluating usability:

- **Inspection-based evaluation:** In these cases an expert evaluates the prototype or final implementation of the user interface according to predefined criteria, which can be a series of properties that must be met (such as providing continuous feedback of the status of the

interaction) or indications of aspects to be considered
by simulating user interaction (such as what occurs
with the cognitive walkthrough).

- **Evaluation based on user tests in the laboratory:** In
  this case, laboratories equipped with cameras store
  user sessions, in an environment that tries to be as
  unobtrusive as possible.

- **Evaluation based on user feedback:** In this
  case, feedback is collected informally through
  questionnaires, workshops, focus groups, and
  interviews.

- **Remote assessment:** The user and the assessor are
  separated in time and/or space, for example, log files of
  interactions with users are automatically created and
  then analyzed using specific tools.

- **Model-based assessment (simulation):** A model is
  created to predict and analyze how tasks are performed
  in a certain interface.

- **Evaluation based on user observation in the field:**
  Users are observed for long periods when interacting
  with the system in their daily environment.

Choosing the method for evaluating usability may depend on various
factors, such as the number and type of users available. It may be useful to
combine multiple methods. For example, starting with an analysis of users
and tasks, then creating prototypes that they may be subjected to heuristic
evaluation, and then using empirical tests until satisfactory results are
achieved.

Bringing Usability and Accessibility Together

If there is no integration between accessibility and usability, there is a risk of having systems that allow access even to disabled users but with difficulty. To better understand these issues, we can take the example of the interaction of blind users through screen readers, devices that convert all the information that is on the screen into voice format. To facilitate interaction, they have commands that allow users, for example, to access the list of links or frames that are on a web page. The accessibility guidelines are applied (for example, those of the W3C), yet various navigation problems may still emerge for users interacting via screen readers:

- **Lack of context in the presentation:** By reading through the screen reader, the user can lose the overall context of the page and read only small portions of text. For example, when moving from one link to another with the Tab key, the blind user reads the link text via the Braille device or listens to it via the speech synthesizer (for example, ".pdf," "more detail," etc.), but does not know the text that is before and after this link.

- **Information overload:** The static portion of the page (link, frame, etc.) can overload the reading through the screen reader because the user must read this part again, even when accessing different pages, thus slowing down navigation.

- **Excessive sequencing in the reading of information:** The commands to navigate and read can force the user to acquire the content of the page sequentially. Therefore, it is important to introduce mechanisms to facilitate the identification of precise parts on the page. An example is the results page generated by a search engine. Usually, in the upper part of such pages, there are several links, advertisements, a search button, and other buttons, and the search results appear below all this.

To overcome these problems, there is a need to identify design criteria which, in addition to ensuring accessibility, also allow for high ease of use when the systems are accessed by disabled users.

Analysis of Task Situations

Two important techniques for analyzing user needs and designing usable systems are scenarios and analysis of tasks. Scenarios are used to understand user behavior in real life. They describe specific users in specific circumstances.

Usually three to four scenarios describe standard users. It is a cheap technique as it does not require excessive effort, but it can be limited when there are many types of users or many possible interactions. It's about a compact and informal description of one or more specific users who interact with a specific interface, to achieve a specific result, in specific circumstances. It is useful for capturing the context in which an application is used, soliciting a discussion that's useful for identifying requirements, capturing important episodes from user behavior studies, and providing a context for carrying out the assessment.

These scenarios can be noted with an indication of the positive and negative consequences deriving from their occurrence. In the analysis of tasks, the activities that must be supported, the objects that are used to perform the activities, the knowledge required to perform the tasks, the possible allocation of tasks between system, and the users are identified.

Various techniques can be used to support the analysis of tasks: interviews or workshops; questionnaires, user observations, analysis of how activities are performed, analysis of existing documentation, and methods of formation. From an analysis of the tasks, it is possible to derive real models that define the semantic relationships and time between tasks. Such descriptions can be used in a complementary way with the scenarios, because the scenarios are informal but detailed descriptions of a specific use in a specific context, whereas the task templates describe the possible activities and their relationships. Scenarios can support the development of task models by indicating part of the activities to be considered and, conversely, there may be scenarios derived from specific sequences of tasks to be performed.

In general, task models can be useful for understanding an application domain, memorizing the result of an interdisciplinary discussion, designing a new application consistent with the user's conceptual model, analyzing and evaluating the usability of an existing application, helping the user during a session with the online help system, and documenting an interactive application.

Techniques and Tools for Human-Computer Interaction Development

All systems design starts with tools and methodologies. Methods might be formal and well-structured, or they can be haphazard and impromptu. Programming languages and advanced software environment that facilitate coding are examples of such tools.

UI architects and developers employ tools and approaches that have been expressly created to create highly useable interfaces. The creation of user interfaces necessitates a consumer or oriented approach in which the system's prospective users engage in some manner in the design and implementation process from the start. As a result, HCI interaction tools and approaches tend to enhance the formulation and construction of interfaces by allowing designers to completely comprehend the primary features of users, such as their tasks, and communicate those traits in a way that aids the development and execution process[3].

In general, HCI tools and methodologies aid programmers in the creation of useable systems. Tools and methodologies can help UI designers create systems that fulfill the demands of users. Furthermore, tools and approaches reduce the amount of work and time necessary to construct the system, which may account for a major portion of the entire effort spent on any system/game's development. This method is also more willing to enable a game's full potential to be appreciated and used, due to its high usefulness. See Figure 1-7.

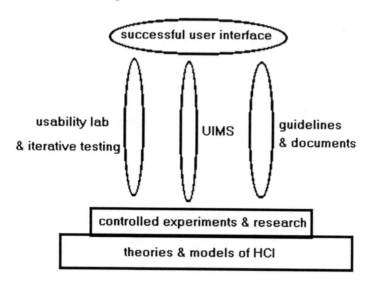

Figure 1-7. *Human-computer interaction design's three cornerstones (usablity, UIMS, and guidelines)*

Tools for HCI development include:

- Tools for description (design), action level, such as Visual Studio

- Building deployment tools, such as Microsoft Visio

- Tools for evaluating, such as IBM tools

Techniques for Defining Specifications

Grammar for many parties:

- Grammar in the style of BNF (Backus normal form).

- The string's non-terminal is labeled by the party that makes it (U:user, C: computer).

- Taking the first steps in a login procedure, for example.

```
<session> --> <u:opening> <c:responding>
<u:opening> --> <login <u:name>
<u:name> --> <u:string>
<c:responding> --> hello [<u:name>]
```

The menu.trees

- At a glance, you can view the complete menu structure.

- It's impossible to illustrate all of the potential user activities (static).

In the diagram of a transition, every conceivable transition is specified (see Figure 1-8).

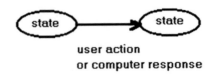

Figure 1-8. *State*

For repeated transitions, a clustering tool can be used to represent state transitions. The cycle is depicted on the left side of Figure 1-8, and the transaction is repeated. State transitions might be represented with the assistance of a clustering tool (such as Azure Stack HCI-certified micro-cluster tool).

The exponent for user activity:

- Interface for direct manipulation.

- For aiming, moving, hitting, and other actions, use a high-level language.

- Task, for example: choose a symbol

user actions
~[icon]Mv   interface feedback
M^   icon!

The depiction based on events

- Utilizing an incident description language for concurrent conversation:

```
event handler event-handler-name IS
token
token-name event-name; /* for I/0 tokens */
var
type variable-name = initial-value;
event event-name: type {
statment }
event event-name: type {
statment }
end event-handler-name;
```

Instruments for implementation include the following:

- Tools for screen mock-ups and modeling, such as specialized prototyping equipment, paper and pencil, word processors, and corporate slide presentation software.

Development tools for coding, such as common widgets: Microsoft's Window Developer's Toolkit, Apple's MacApp, Unix's Xtk, etc.

- UIMS, such as elevated specs for user interface designer (without coding) ---> UI open source.

Instruments for assessment include the following:

- Examine if the menu tree is too deep, whether widget names are utilized consistently, and whether all icons have corrected transitions, among other things.

- Operated logging software records a user's activity patterns.

Problems in selecting computer software include the following:

- Panels, dialog boxes, pull-down and pop-up menus, buttons, navigation bars, metadata, column labels, sliders, and other widgets are allowed.

- Color, images, pictures, animations, video, variable display size, audio, music, speech input/output, mouse, directional buttons, touchscreen, stylus are all aspects of the UI.

- UIMS, description technique (CMD language, menus, form, manipulation of objects), degrees and severity of user-interface reliance, computer program, evaluation and documenting tools, interface with database, graphics, network, spreadsheets, logs during test and usage.

- Managerial concerns include the amount of pleased tool users, vendor dependability and scalability, pricing, paperwork, training, and tech assistance, and program management assistance.

The following components can be used to assess user experience:

- **Effectiveness:** Will ordinary users be able to perform their work? Will the system cater to a wide range of user abilities and requirements?

- **Learnability:** Is it easy to understand how to run the machine? How simple will it be to reenter the system? How much information will be usable in other processes?

- **Flexibility:** Is it easy to edit the system without making it less user-friendly?

- **Attitude:** Is the system easy and enjoyable to use?

The Cycle of Tool Life and Methodologies Taxonomy

Incremental prototypes with considerable, early, and ongoing user feedback is common in the creation of user interfaces. The four major stages of the software development process are as follows[3]:

1. Define and analyze user needs.

2. Define the layout and the system requirements.

3. Construct and evaluate the design.

Delivery and upkeep are the fourth and fifth steps, as shown in Figure 1-9.

Figure 1-9. *Product development steps*

These are arbitrary categorizations that do not represent iterations or progress, but they serve as a starting point for tools and processes. Specific tools and/or procedures associated with each phase have been created specifically for use in that sector. Samples of significant tools and procedures related to each area will be included in the discussion.

The majority of instruments are applications that are useful for a range of hardware, including IBM PCs and motherboard chipsets, as well as Unix workstations. Apple Macs and NeXT computers are two different types of computers. Overall, HCI software-based solutions have been designed for commercial usage and, as a result, have been evaluated in real-world scenarios.[3]

When compared to tools, HCI techniques often entail pencil and paper procedures (although some methods may use computer software) and are frequently more exploratory and scholarly in character. HCI methods are frequently designed by professionals for use in labs, making them more difficult to apply unless you have experience with HCI and usability engineering.

Depending on the system being developed and the stage of the software development cycle, different tools and approaches will be used.

Selecting Instruments, Techniques, and Resources

Selecting instruments and/or approaches can be difficult, especially for those who are unskilled. Data systems, special interests, human-computer interaction publications, regulations, and confidentiality procedures are some of the information sources available. HCI techniques and approaches are becoming increasingly crucial in the creation of user

---

[3] P. O'Brian Holt, "HCI tools, methods and information sources," IEE Colloquium on Usability Now, 1991, pp. 5/1-5/2.

interface design, and there is no doubt that they play a substantial role in achieving high usability. The variety of tools and approaches available, as well as their varying intricacy and complexities, may provide a barrier in terms of selection and use. However, there are now standards for selecting and using these tools and procedures.

To have an effective HCI, you need to have effective eye-tracking methodologies. Eye movements are considered a critical real-time input channel for HCI, which really is especially significant for persons with disabilities. By relying on the user's vision, the suggested method aims to provide an easy and practical interaction approach. The next section discusses how eye tracking helps in HCI.

The Eye Tracking Technique and Usability

Eye tracking is a new form of interaction between human and machine. The combination of infrared lighting and cameras provides the basis for a wide range of interactive techniques in which a device can "see" the users and interpret their intentions.

The act of detecting which region of an application or website somebody is looking at, or (more precisely), how the eyes move in respect to the head, is known as eye tracking. It offers previously unavailable insights about your customers and enables a new degree of knowledge of the interaction between consumers and interfaces.

On mobile devices, the majority of customer interaction takes the form of tapping, swiping, and scrolling. These trends provide you with essential information about your consumers. However, when there is no physical connection, such as when somebody is viewing a text, things get complicated. These user habits are rather prevalent, if we think about it.

In the feared circumstance where people report they "simply don't understand it," eye tracking can assist. It might be difficult to figure out what went wrong if there was no physical connection. It's possible that the person is perplexed, searching for something, or just stopped. Whatever it is, eye tracking technologies that emphasizes where the user is looking might convey that "why."

Eye Tracking Studies

Eye tracking studies are most commonly connected with assessing what grabs the user's attention, and this is a common outcome of a research study. Human eye gaze research has been around for a long time. Eye motions were studied in the 19th Century by direct observation of people, such as when they read books. The individual eye's movement is revealed to be a sequence of small pauses, known as *fixations*, rather than a continuous journey. Our mind then stitches various fixings together to form a seamless picture. Fascinations are what we're most interested in in usability testing

Fixations are frequently depicted as circles in gaze tracking studies. The larger the circle, the greater the concentration.

Whenever we come upon anything intriguing, we become fixated on it. This might happen intentionally (when we're seeking for something specific) or subconsciously (since we're caught off guard). Nevertheless, concentration provides knowledge of human conduct by revealing what qualities attract our attention.

Eye monitoring investigations are most typically associated with determining what attracts user attention, and this is a common consequence of a research. However, there's more to it: eye tracking can also help you grasp things more deeply.

User Control

We are often referred to be operating in the economic market, as you may have heard. Interest, according to marketing methods like the AIDA model, is the important first step in the process of purchasing a product. The activity is at the bottom of the funnel. This is the point at which we make a commitment by buying a product or subscribing to a magazine.

Interest and desire are the phases between attention and action in the AIDA paradigm (see Figure 1-10). This is when we look into it and decide whether it's what we really want. To put it another way, this is the point at which the users make a decision.

Figure 1-10. *The AIDA analysis is a good way of describing the phases that go from attention to action*

Letting people make their own decisions means giving them control. Allowing this sense of power, according to recent UX trends, seems to be something we'll see much more in the future. People have become more aware of how their digital experiences affect them, and their (often harmful) digital conduct is being called into question. Customers no longer want to be controlled by their smartphones and digital services, according to tools that limit screen time or include snooze functionality.

The problem with commerce is that getting people to take action (this usually means purchasing a product) is clearly relevant to the organization's growth. Relevant stakeholders, unsurprisingly, want their users to take action as soon as feasible. The issue is that if we aggressively shrink the space between attention and action, we start to take away user control. For example, one-click checkout buttons are convenient and beneficial to your organization, but they also raise the chance of your customers buying stuff they aren't convinced about, or worse, purchasing things by accident.

Usability Testing

Testing via eye tracking is extremely valuable, providing you with an additional layer of information about your users' behavior. Even so, it's critical to understand when you should employ eye tracking and when you can't do anything without it. Regardless of how advanced the technology is, it should be considered a tool in your usability testing toolbox rather than a UX panacea. When it comes to user testing, a general rule of thumb is to try to get your answers as quickly as possible. Don't go overboard.

Why Eye Tracking?

As a user experience designer, you may need to defend your design decisions on occasion. Because your work is available to everybody, everybody will have an opinion about it. Eye tracking may help you justify your design choices and is a great approach to take the "I" out of the equation—the users' actions speak for themselves. Demonstrating that you picked a particular color or interface element to better the customer experience strengthens your position in these instances.

Incorporating eye-tracking technology into your usability studies may help you create better, more natural customer experiences, when it's done correctly.

Creating an Effective Interface

Web designers, software developers, and all those who are studying to become such, will sooner or later come across the expression "graphic interface". Related abbreviations, such as UI, TUI (Text User Interface), and GUI (Graphical User Interface) are also often used. It's of fundamental importance for a good user experience, whether on a website, app, or software.

The user interface includes all the tools that the user sees and uses to perform actions, ranging from simple text-based command lines to complicated structures of graphical interfaces. At the same time, the UI causes the machine to send feedback to the users so that they know that their actions have been carried out successfully. The user interface is closely linked to usability. For some time now, it has no longer been exclusively a question of creating an interface that is purely functional: now even the aesthetic aspects are increasingly important. Equally essential is ensuring a good user experience; the entire experience that a user has when visiting a website or using software. The goal of every web designer is therefore to lay the foundations for a good user experience by creating an intuitive UI. Normally, this works best through a graphical interface, but other innovative types of UI also work to lighten the interaction with computers and other devices.

More and more advanced methods have been developed to allow interaction between humans and machines. In fact, today there are many different types of user interfaces. At the beginning of this evolution there were the simple command-line interfaces (CLI), but numerous technical innovations have led to a more immediate and direct usability, called the Natural User Interfaces (NUI). There is even the use of devices for measuring brain activity (EEGs, or "electroencephalograms"), which are increasingly being researched. The next section introduces the UIs that stand out and summarizes their main features.

Graphical User Interfaces

Graphical user interfaces are the standard nowadays. They can be used through control elements and symbols, inspired by objects in the real world. Users typically use a mouse and keyboard as the control tools, but increasingly they are also using touchscreen sensors that react to contact. Together with the graphic interface, icons also enter the digital world, just like individual windows and the trashcan. With the mouse, or by touching the touchscreen, desired elements are selected and opened with a simple click. The graphic design is oriented toward the traditional office environment.

The consequence is that all the elements are easily identifiable, and the operations are performed in a more intuitive way than from the command list of the command-line interface. Even inexperienced users will immediately understand the functions of the icons: they don't need additional explanation to be understood. Meanwhile this form of symbolism has become the standard for UIs, just like GUIs themselves. In fact, there is no graphics program whose tool icons do not refer to objects in the real world, including the brush, the pen, and the eraser.

Characteristics of User Interfaces

Every web designer and software developer should deal in depth with the topic of UI. If you intend to entice users with your app, website, or online store, you have to structure your site properly and produce it in the most intuitive and simple way possible.

For this reason, it is first of all essential to precisely identify your target audience. The design of the UI should be customized according to this target. As a rule, you have to focus on the graphical interface— functionality, ease of use, and aesthetics are the criteria for a good user experience. You must never lose sight of the usability factor. If an app is difficult to use, not even an attractive design will be enough to convince the users to use it.

To optimize your website or app, it is essential to carry out detailed tests. User studies can provide useful results, thanks to the analysis by means of a heatmap. In using a heatmap, usability is displayed: user behavior is reconstructed by means of the tracking of clicks, scrolls, and mouse or eye movement, and subsequently rendered with color gradations.

Only in the second step does it come to aesthetics. Here the motto reigns: "less is more". The design must support the functionality of the graphical interface. Consequently, the structure must be clear and well organized. This does not mean that designers cannot indulge themselves: the important thing is to know the target's usage habits, without limiting functionality with design.

But why are intuitive UIs so important? Let's try to clarify it using an example: the symbol of a butterfly can be beautiful and with a certain probability it will also appeal to one target or another. But if it is used as an icon for the Save button, the program will have to pay the consequences of the design, since practically no one associates a butterfly with the memorization process. Instead, the choice of a disk as an icon is understood. Even if the medium depicted is now obsolete, it will always be used as a symbol for the storage process.

Users expect to see this symbol and look for it almost instinctively, as is the case with other standard icons. Consequently, to plan a good user experience and an intuitively understandable graphical interface, the symbolic conventions in use should be taken into consideration.

The web designer/software developer must always find the balance between aesthetics and functionality to be successful. UI optimization is essential to guarantee the users the best possible experience.

Finally, depending on the orientation of the website or software, this leads to more conversions, recommendations, and a marketing of the viral product, therefore supported by the customer. In addition to the GUI, it is also worthwhile to integrate additional user interfaces. If for example it is possible to use voice control with an app or if a notebook also works with the touchscreen, the result will be greater accessibility and will lead to a better user experience. This gives users a wider variety of possibilities to use the product. This means that there is more flexibility and that the range of action of the app and product increases.

Summary

The game interface, as well as the principles of HCI tools and techniques, were covered in this chapter. These notions serve as the foundation for the following chapter, which focuses on the use of eye tracking when creating apps and software. The following chapter shows you how to use HCI approaches to create effective web applications and video games.

CHAPTER 2

Human-Computer Interaction Tools and Game Development

As digital technology advances, increasingly complex video games are being brought to market. As this occurs, interface design becomes increasingly important. This chapter explores how to use HCI design in video game user interfaces to meet the game's HCI needs.

The user interaction in a game needs to be consistent in order to provide an intuitive and enjoyable interface. Consider the method in which individuals play the game. If a regularly-used button appears first at the top-left corner and then in the bottom-right corner in the following level, and finally in the top-right corner again, the players will be confused.

The use of color and whitespace should be uniform as well. It's best to stick to a limited color pallet of primary and secondary hues. Make sure there's a nice contrast between the darker and lighter colors. Lastly, use green for items that provide positive feedback and red for components that provide cautions, notices, and bad reviews. During the game development process, the interface is active. A decent gameplay experience and efficient HCI determine a successful video game user interface.

This chapter also covers on effective eye-tracking tools used in the development of web applications.

J. T. George and M. J. George, *Human-Computer Interaction in Game Development with Python*, https://doi.org/10.1007/978-1-4842-8182-6_2

Tools and Techniques for General Game Development

There are a number of core tools and techniques needed for successful game development, as discussed in the following sections.

The Video Game Interface

The object of computer video games is to give players immersive experiences that include challenges of increasing difficulty. Games must develop victory requirements in order for these difficulties to have genuine value, and these qualities of the game environment are exhibited in front of consumers, thanks to the user interfaces. Game development starts with the design and creation of the game environment. A range of actual locations may be simulated for video games, and certain areas that defy thermodynamics may even be shown through the gaming interface. In some cases, the gaming environment will restrict the user's actions.

Video Game Development and Interaction

The structuring of interaction techniques and procedures between two distinct objects is known as a user interface. It's a method for improving the human-computer interaction connection. The interaction design incorporates engaging, diversified, and near technologies in order to simplify operations and increase the efficiency of human-computer connection. Relevance as well as other aspects are important. The rise of the video game industry has resulted in the creation of game interaction design.

Video Game Users' Requirements and Needs

The goal of user interface design is to make the user's interaction more efficient, so that the player only experiences the game's amusement instead of noticing the actual interface's presence. Actual interface presence may occasionally provide players with experience and feedback about their activities (for example, a win or lose screen or a reward interface).

The social aspect that games embody is at the heart of their existence as a source of entertainment and interaction. Users will have various experiences depending on the sort of game they are playing. As the narrative unfolds, gamers seek to fully immerse themselves in the gaming environment and attain a sense of completion. Of course, if you want to improve the game's playability even more, you may include more interactive features in the procedure. When players enter a video game, they enter an autonomous digital reality, as if they were in a dream world and were the ruler of this universe to some extent. In the game, players must use their minds to complete specific tasks. Diverse forms of games elicit different emotions in individuals, both dynamic and static, and cater to the requirements of diverse types of people.

In most cases, to varying degrees, the gaming world is a virtual representation of the actual world. It is the gaming player's expectation that the game will indicate which procedures are achievable and show the outcomes in a virtual world, with the support of the game user's real-world experience.

The video game is a whole story in which players immerse themselves, investigate step by step, and aspire to build their own successful tales. As a result, the user interface must be separated into categories, well structured, and finished effectively as a game player. The true guide of the game is the player, who mixes everyday life experiences with game instructions, arouses the inner self, and introduces creativity into the game.

Failure is unavoidable during the gameplay, which leads to a recurring issue. Repetition is another important aspect in several games. Sport and competitive games, such as Tetris and the Need for Speed, might always offer a varied result experience with each repeat. Every time a user plays the game, it is repeated. Everyone can have distinct sensations and have different "interactions" that are comparable to that person's real life.

Interactive UI Design for a Game

The computer coding language behind the computer monitor is the main body of the game, but the tasks performed by this code are presented on the computer monitor. HCI must be founded on technological feasibility and naturally combined with the subtle aesthetic qualities that appeal to gamers. Conversation design, menu item design, panel design, symbol design, and coloring design are only a few of the core duties of gaming user interfaces.

Contact is founded on "conversation." Developing objectives, forming intents, defining actions, carrying out tasks, knowing system status, and informing the system are all phases of the user's man-machine communication in the game. There are seven phases in all, including the current stage and the findings of the evaluation. In these phases, the dialogue between the user and the machine proceeds in order.

Different strategies must be examined in order to complete the interpersonal interactions at various phases. As illustrated in Table 2-1, there are five types of methodologies: panel selection, form, CMD language, natural language, and direct action. Each technique has its own qualities and understanding how to coordinate their use in user interfaces is crucial to creating successful communications (see Table 2-1).

Table 2-1. *The Five Different Person Conversation Modes*

Conversation	Advantages	Drawbacks
Panel selection	The learning is quick, the click-through rate is low, and the architecture is straightforward, making mistake management easy.	The operating performance of a higher-frequency players is slowed by poor menu detection. However, it may not be suitable for small display size devices.
Forms	Simplify administration, make comparisons easier, and therefore only require a modest bit of assistance.	Inputting data is time-consuming, which is detrimental to the player's consistency.
CMD language	Frequent players will find this versatile and appealing. Applaud the commitment of the player.	It's not simple to get the word out. It takes a lot of practice and memorization. Inadequate error management abilities.
Natural language	Making it natural is important for the better interaction for players/users.	It has some technical challenges to make it natural.
Direct action	Visualize jobs to make it easier to understand and prevent mistakes.	The complexity of coding. Management of multi-device usage.

When it comes to conversation design, several rules should be observed in addition to comprehending the fundamental conversation approaches. Figure 2-1 depicts the particular guidelines.

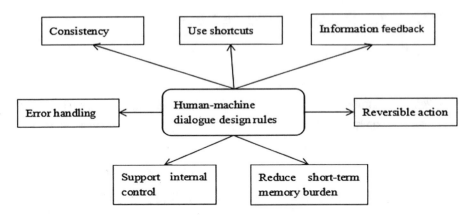

Figure 2-1. *Design guidelines for human-machine communication*

Panel Design

The fundamental goal of panel design is to create a practical and simple semantic structure that meets the gaming task's needs. The most common discretization is detailed breakdown. The matching group is carried out according to the terms of occurrence of use or significance to sort the options, so that the gaming menu functionality is easy to comprehend, according to linguistic classification.

The manner in which the menu is used in the game is determined by the circumstances. Many panel selections need more than one frame of the display screen; however, only one of the alternatives can be selected. To prevent customers from having to hunt for it step by step in complicated menu options, use a forest menu and try to utilize the first tree. In some video games, it's vital to keep some actions on the screen at all times so that they can be called at any moment. This sort of menu is known as a persistent panel, and its design style should be quite similar to that of the games.

Most panel options are put into words, and the architecture should be as simple as possible to comprehend. Pay more attention to the phrasing, so that it's precise and exact, and simple to differentiate. If it's an English panel, the key choice should be placed in the first place to meet most people's reading habits, which are left to right. The menu's general layout should match the game's style and interface design, and the beginning position should be indicated using clear symbols, phrases, or figures.

Window Architecture

The video game is a giant window in itself, and the window architecture is the structuring and organization of its primary features and elements.

- **Title:** Every window should have its own name and be identified in the gameplay with particular symbols and typography.

- **Scroll bar and window panels:** These are solid design elements that can be utilized in the gaming UI and can be easily altered under the concept of maintaining a consistent design.

- **You can enter, shut, resize, and change the size and location of your windows:** The majority of the player's open windows are controlled by push buttons, which are quite fast. The location and width of the windows, as well as the game's own parameters, are primarily designed to fit the demands of users who are "viewing" rather than "creating."

- **Job connection and window architecture:** Due to the need to present game data, two or more windows are frequently displayed. Multi-windows must be designed to meet all of the criteria of a one window, while also taking into account multi-window registrations and synchronization. The gaming interface should present consumers with a clear picture and only a few options.

- **Sliding that is synchronized:** This is fundamental to linking mode. The operations of the two windows are intertwined and changing the contents of one window will modify the contents of the other.

- **Yield components with the best method:** This is a common strategy. When the player moves the mouse over an item, for example, various parameter information about it appears immediately.

- **Browse in two dimensions:** It's perfect for a play of mapping sceneries. The general view of a map or chart is displayed in one frame, and the details are displayed in another bigger window. The user may work on both the large and mini maps.

- **The related window is opened and closed:** Sometimes, one window cannot show all of the player's characteristics entirely, necessitating the classification of this data and its inclusion in a primary screen. The user can use the mouse to open the appropriate panel for viewing. Each window may be retrieved and activated independently. At the same time, these windows are developed in a variety of forms to suit various sorts, comparisons, and ease of reading.

Icon Design

The architecture of an icon may be revealed, the connection expressed, and the unique aesthetic features displayed. It has apparent advantages over other logical and textual phrases, and it can draw players' discussion activities. Since individuals have diverse cognitive types and individual interests, several interface styles are required. Among these, the icon plays a crucial function. It employs graphic elements to plan and process data while also influencing the player's viewing effect in image, picture, and colors.

Symbol design standards—symbols must adhere to people's cognitive patterns and specific design, such as representing things or activities in a common and recognized manner, allowing the icon to stand out against the context. Three-dimensional symbols are more appealing, but when used incorrectly, they may be distracting. It's simple to confuse consumers; make sure that a selected symbol stands out from other icons.

Many aspects of icons are included in video games, and owing to the need for a customized user, icon development in gaming interfaces is somewhat unrestricted. It may be viewed more from a semantics and functional standpoint. The semantics level, for instance, can convey items in tangible, conceptual, component, and practical terms, while the operational level should be ubiquitous and easy to identify and recall.

Color Development

Colors not only draws gamers into the gaming UI, but it also aids in job completion. Color development in video games has no set guidelines, and various people use varying personal styles and interpretations. When colors are used correctly and effectively, they enhance the game's experience.

- **Arrangement of colors:** The colors satisfy the demands of the play style while also achieving coherence between brand recognition and gaming experiences.

- **Keep the number of different colors to a minimum:** Because a computer screen can generate millions and millions of hues, game designers will no longer require as many. Choose wisely based on the type of game and target audience.

- **Its color feature is programmable:** Colors may be used to speed up identification of traits, and various colors can be used to designate phrases or categories in human-computer discourse, which is a successful technique of HCI.

- **The color is chosen by the user:** Users can select colors on their own to improve their involvement and enjoyment.

- **The color scheme is constant during gameplay:** The very same color-coded standards must be applied across systems, and the colors presented in the conversation must be set consistently, which also meets the consistent requirements.

- **A shift in colors implies a change in status:** In action games, this is more visible. A transition from orange to red indicates when the speed is greater than the posted speed, while a gradient from yellow to green indicates when the rate is less than the speed limit or very sluggish.

Because computing technologies are constantly evolving, game interface design has even more possibilities. In the advancement of computer video games, increasing the HC performance is an unavoidable tendency.

We believe that video games will become more immersive, that they will integrate into society, and that they will become an indispensable part of people's lives. The technique known as *eye tracking* is essential for creating a successful gaming interface; the following section focuses on this topic.

Eye-Tracking Techniques

The Impact of Eye Tracking in Games

Computers can comprehend what players are glancing at by using an eye tracker. Eye-tracking technology can enhance the gaming experience and allow you to use natural eye movements in combination with keyboards, mice, and analog joysticks as an extra input.

This and the following chapter create an algorithm for the approximate tracking of the direction of the human gaze using the camera of common smartphones. Currently there are various eye-tracking technologies at various levels of precision, almost always based on expensive, dedicated hardware. The ultimate goal is to integrate the algorithm into smartphone apps and allow those who are using it to be alerted if someone peeks into their device.

The basic idea is to use the user's front camera to "intercept" and analyze the eye movements of the various framed faces, excluding the user's face and using functions already present in Android. The algorithm aims to provide an alert if it detects prying glances at your smartphone and solicit privacy protection behavior, for example, by avoiding reading sensitive data or typing passwords.

Eye Tracking in Games

The relationship between the movements of the human eye and the emotions they convey is a subject of interest since ancient times and of great interest to social and behavioral psychology. With the advancement of technology and detection techniques, medicine has also begun to nurture a strong interest in data relating to eye movements and consider them as a support tool for the diagnosis of some pathologies.

45

Obviously, the first forms of detection were of the visual type, which were followed at the end of the 19th Century by experiments with particular contact lenses connected to instruments that detected eye movements. In the first decades of the 20th Century, the first non-intrusive detection techniques were invented, through the light reflected by the pupils, with the aim of studying the strategies that the eye uses to read a written text or image.

The medical scientific terminology that characterizes the field of study is not the subject of this study; however, it is good to clarify some key concepts that are the basis of even the most sophisticated modern techniques of eyes tracking. The observation of eye movements, the contraction and dilation of the pupils, were born in a clinical-medical context with the aim of understanding the functioning of the complex system of human vision.

Light penetrates inside the eye through the pupil and hits the receptors in the retina, which then transmit information to the brain. In reality, only the central part of the retina, the fovea, is able to see the image clearly. The rest of the retina perceives the image as far as it is from the fovea. In order to allow the brain to reconstruct the focused image in its entirety, the eye constantly makes micro movements. At the end of each movement, a so-called crossing takes place, lasting 2-4 seconds. This movement occurs with a frequency of 3-4 movements per second. Unlike voluntary eye movement, which each of us makes to direct our gaze where we want, this movement is involuntary.

The pupil dilation and contraction mechanism, directly related to the autonomic nervous system and therefore also of an involuntary nature, has the main function of filtering the amount of light necessary for correct vision. Therefore, it expands with darkness and shrinks when there is a lot of light. Furthermore, alongside this linear filter function, the pupils can have similar behaviors in emotional and/or pathological situations, therefore this is a source of valuable information for the observer. It is precisely the relationship between eye movements and the emotional sphere that has in fact expanded the sectors that are interested in the data provided by the eye movement detection.

We can learn more about a new eye-tracking technology that can employ cameras for business purposes without needing specialized gear. We learn more about these issues in the following sections.

Project Planning and Development

The goal of this study is to create an eye-tracking device that uses cameras for commercial use without needing specific hardware. For example, you can use the webcams integrated in PCs or smartphones. I structured the presentation by dedicating a section to each test in order to detail the procedure used and explain the processes that determined the final choice.

Development Environment

The Python language was used to create the application. The main reason that this language was chosen is for its portability and for the possibility of developing at a high level. In addition, the numerous libraries and tools represent a further element of advantage. The application was developed in the Unix environment, using `sublime-text`[1, 2] as the editor, in particular the main library used and OpenCV.

OpenCV

OpenCV (Open-Source Computer Vision Library) was released under a BSD and therefore Open-Source license for both academic and commercial use. It has C ++, Python, and Java interfaces and supports

---

[1]`https://www.sublimetext.com/`
[2]`https://opencv.org/`

Windows, Linux, macOS, iOS, and Android. OpenCV was designed for computational efficiency and with a strong focus on real-time applications. Written in C/C++, the library can take advantage of multi-core processing. Enabled with OpenCL, it can take advantage of the hardware acceleration of the underlying heterogeneous computing platform (see Figure 2-2).

Adopted all over the world, OpenCV has a community of over 47,000 users and an estimated number of downloads exceeding 14 million. Uses range from interactive art to mine inspection, to point maps on the web and advanced robotics.

Structure of OpenCV

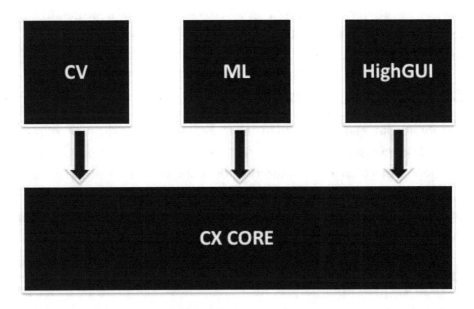

Figure 2-2. Structure of OpenCV[3]

---

[3]https://www.domsoria.com/2018/05/face-recognition-and-tracking-con-opencv-prima-parte/

- CXCORE: Implements data structures and functions to manage images and videos.

- CV: Module specialized in image processing and analysis, calibration, and tracking.

- ML (Machine Learning): Contains many features on Machine Learning and pattern recognition, such as clustering and classification.

- HighGUI: Implements the definitions of user interfaces (GUI).

During installation, the numpy library is also required (this is a very powerful mathematical library that speeds up real-time calculations).

OpenCV was used to recognize, in the first phase, the face and eyes taken from a photo. In the second phase, it was used to track the movements of the pupil. Everything was created using the framework functions that are used to recognize objects in an image through the "haar cascade."

Haar Cascade

This is basically a classifier that is used to detect the object for which it was trained, from the source. The technology is based on superimposing the positive image on a series of negative images. Training (classification) consists of collecting data of an object that you subsequently want to recognize. To have optimal results, a large amount of data (high-resolution images) of the object is required. On GitHub[4], there are several HaarCascade options that can be downloaded and used.

---

[4]https://github.com/opencv/opencv/tree/master/data/haarcascades

Face and Eye Recognition

The goal of this algorithm is to recognize, through the computer's camera, if there are faces and eyes and highlight the results on the screen.

Modeling and Development

Initially, the recognition algorithm was focused on two points:

- Face recognition

- Eye recognition

The first tests were carried out on various images of type JPEG and PNG "with different subjects and one or more faces in the same image." After obtaining positive results with images, the next step was the transition to a video input in real-time, showing the results on-screen with blue rectangles for the faces and red for the eyes (see Figure 2-3).

Figure 2-3. *Application screenshot*

Here is the Python algorithm used for recognition. This code's fundamental phases are as follows:

1. Imagine the background color

2. Face recognition

3. x, y coordinates of the upper-left point - w, h width and height

4. Eye recognition

5. Add the red rectangle

Note   This project used the OpenCV-Python library. The Open CV-Python is a Python binding library for solving computer vision challenges. Numpy, a highly efficient library for numerical operations with a MATLAB-style syntax, is used by OpenCV-Python. All array structures in OpenCV are translated to and from Numpy arrays.

In this project we are also using graphs so we can understand tracking methods easily. Plotting graphs in Python might be difficult, but a few easy steps can help you build a graph. To create graphs in Python, you need the Matplotlib package. It makes it easy to see the link between various factors. Before beginning the graph, it is critical to first comprehend Matplotlib and its Python methods.

The first step is to use the `pip` command to install Matplotlib.

```
pip install matplotlib
```

This will take care of dependencies while installing the library in Python using the `pip` function. You may be expecting that to begin plotting graphs in Python, there will be certain standard commands that you will use to make graphs. Matplotlib has greatly reduced that work by providing a configurable package with many built-in settings for quickly creating graphs.

The source code can be found here:

`https://github.com/JosephThachilGeorge/GameEyeTracking`

Listing 2-1. Python Algorithm Used for Recognition

```python
import numpy as np
import cv2

face_cascade = cv2 . CascadeClassifier ('
haarcascade_frontalface_default .xml ')
cap = cv2 . VideoCapture (0)

while 1:

# imagine

ret , img = cap . read ()

if ret == True :
gray = cv2 . cvtColor ( img , cv2 . COLOR_BGR2GRAY )
```

```python
# face recognition

faces = face_cascade . detectMultiScale ( gray , 1.3 , 5)
eye_cascade = cv2 . CascadeClassifier (' haarcascade_
eye . xml '
)
eyes = eye_cascade . detectMultiScale ( img ,1.3 ,10)

for (x ,y ,w , h ) in faces :
# x, y coordinates of the upper left point - w, h width
and height

cv2 . rectangle ( img ,( x , y ) ,( x +w , y + h ) ,(255
,0 ,0) ,2)

#blue rectangle
#eye recognition

for ( ex , ey , ew , eh ) in eyes :

#ex, ey, top left point coordinates - ew, eh width and height

cv2 . rectangle ( img , ( ex , ey ) , (( ex + ew ) ,( ey +
eh ) ) ,
(0 ,0 ,255) ,1)

# red rectangle

cv2 . line ( img , ( ex , ey ) , (( ex + ew , ey + eh ) ) , (0
,0 ,255) ,1)
#line for x
cv2 . line ( img , ( ex + ew , ey ) , (( ex , ey + eh ) ) , (0
,0 ,255) ,1)

#line for x
cv2 . imshow ('img ', img )
```

```
k = cv2 . waitKey (30) & 0 xff
if k == ord ('q') :
break

cap . release ()
cv2 . destroyAllWindows ()
```

Conclusions and Problems

In most cases, the recognition is precise and the eyes and faces are correctly identified. However, there are cases of recognition of objects outside the face that are not eyes. In addition, if the subject moves quickly, this creates instability in the algorithm that recognizes the eyes and face with an immediate effect.

Creating the Data Structure

Since in various cases the OpenCV framework mistakenly recognizes objects or shapes as eyes, this data structure aims to create a cache with the history of the last "n" positions in order to avoid errors.

Modeling and Development

A data structure was created in order to allow the analysis of the last positions of an eye. To build the data structure, different classes were created for the face and eyes. The data is saved in two arrays containing the data of the respective classes.

The classes therefore contain the coordinates of the recognized object and a value called "priority". Priority is used to determine if and when an object can be considered new, old, or a false positive. For each object recognized in a frame of the video, a search is carried out in the data structure. If the object was already present (with a fixed or set) the data structure is updated; otherwise, it is added to a temporary data structure to be evaluated later. The movement of an object, from the temporary to the actual data structure, occurs when this object appears at least in "n" frames, thus reaching a higher "priority".

Conclusions and Problems

Eye recognition is more precise, to the detriment of speed. Rapid movements struggle to associate the eye with its respective history present in the data structure; however, errors and false positives have been significantly reduced. Some of the errors, which are still numerous, are attributable to the alterations of light and colors present in an RGB image and to the "forcing" recognition of the eye.

Applying Photographic Filters

The objective here is to reduce image noise in order to improve recognition of various environmental conditions such as brightness, contrast, exposure, etc.

Modeling and Development

The colors of an image are not useful for eye recognition. We therefore prefer to use as input images in shades of gray. Once the image has been modified, the photographic filter has been applied.

Gaussian Blur is an image processing based on a mathematical formula, Gaussian, which reduces image noise. The visual effect of this technique is a homogeneous blur. Figure 2-4 shows two examples of images with this filter applied.

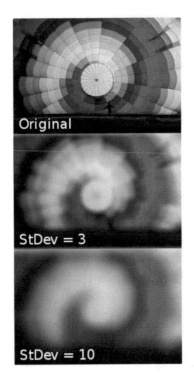 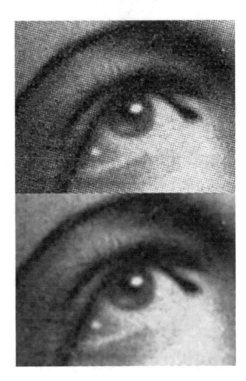

Figure 2-4. *Examples of the Gaussian Blur filter*

Conclusions

The image noise has been significantly reduced. Face recognition was removed during development because it is not useful for the algorithm. In particular, the case of a subject looking at the camera without his face being entirely framed is a criticism.

Recognizing the Iris

The object is to geometrically recognize the position of the iris in the eye.

Modeling and Development

To determine the direction of the gaze, it is necessary to search for the iris. To achieve this goal, the OpenCV HoughCircles function was used, which allows you to search for circles in a given image. Specifically, "n" images were created, as many as there are eyes in the data structure, in such a way as to limit the search to the geometric shape of the circle that corresponds to the shape of the iris or pupil (see Figure 2-5).

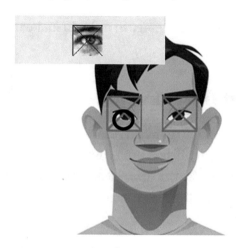

Figure 2-5. *Application screenshot*

Conclusions and Problems

As you can also see from the image, the recognition is not entirely accurate. The error is mainly determined by two factors:

- The iris is not always perfectly circular. It may be covered by the upper or lower eyelid.

- Pattern recognition (of the HoughCircle function) is not efficient due to a large amount of pixels to be analyzed; consequentially the results are unstable.

The first problem can be solved by instructing the algorithm to search for an elliptical shape (eyeball) and then for the circle of the pupil, but unfortunately OpenCV does not allow the search of an ellipse as a geometric shape. Consequently it is not possible to specifically identify the contours of the sclera.

Edge Detection

The objective is to "clean" the image in order to make the recognition of the iris more effective.

Modeling and Development

Specific filters were applied to "clean" the image, particularly suitable for minimizing noise and highlighting the contours of the sclera and iris. This makes it easier to search for the desired shapes as the recognized outlines most pertinent to reality. The effects used, in addition to the blur, are CLAHE and CANNY.

- **CLAHE (Contrast Limited Adaptive Histogram Equalization):** An adaptive histogram equalization is a digital image processing technique used to improve contrast. It differs from the ordinary equalization of the histogram since the suitable method calculates different histograms, each corresponding to a distinct section of the image, and uses them to distribute the brightness values. It is can also be used to enhance the local contrast of an image and add more detail (see Figure 2-6).

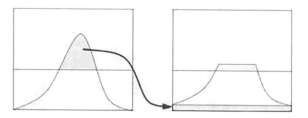

Figure 2-6. *Adaptive equalization of the histogram*

- **CANNY:** CANNY's algorithm is an operator for the recognition of contours (edge detection) conceived in 1986 by John F. Canny. It uses a multi-stage calculation method for identifying outlines of many of the types normally found in real pictures (see Figure 2-7).

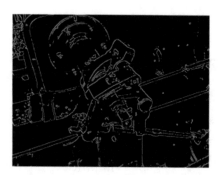

Figure 2-7. *An example of the CANNY filter*

The inclusion of these two additional effects made it possible to make the image of the eye sharper and enhance the identification of the contours, as shown in Figure 2-8.

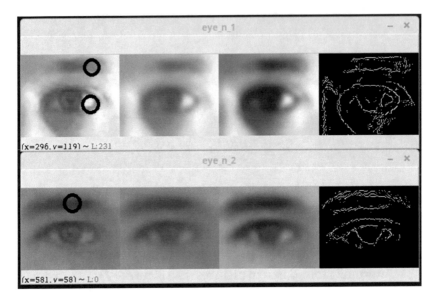

Figure 2-8. *Image of the eye sharpener*

Conclusions and Problems

Once the effects are applied, the recognized edges are faithful to reality. The main problem, which is also shown in the figure, denotes that there is a lot of difference between the results in relation to the parameters used to calibrate the effects. Consequently, the recognition is incorrect in some case studies. Moreover, the final result is strongly conditioned by elements external such as brightness, contrast, colors, etc.

Parameter Analysis on Blur, CLAHE, and CANNY Filters

The different possible combinations of the various photographic filters have a significant influence on the final result. The goal of this phase was to structure this information and establish numerical ranges that could increase the efficiency of recognition.

Modeling and Development

In this phase, I focused my attention on the attributes and parameters of the effects, by studying the trend of results as one or more parameters vary. To do this, the following steps were carried out:

1. Record the video with different brightness and contrast.

2. Save the position of the real iris.

3. Recognize the position of the iris by means of an algorithm by varying the parameters of the effects.

4. Save the data in CSV format.

5. Perform graphical data analysis.

A considerable amount of graphics have been generated, thanks to the use of R, which made it possible to analyze the relationships between the various filters and choose the best parameters.

Listing 2-2. Generating the Graphs

```
1    library ( ggplot2 )
2
3 colnames <- c('CN1 ','CN2 ','BL1 ','BL2 ','CL ','PP1 ','PP2
','FRAME
','ES ','ER ')
4 df <- read .csv ('es.csv ', col . names = colnames )
5 summary (df)
6 df$P_ES = df$ES/(df$ FRAME * 2)
7
8 g <- ggplot ( data = df[df$CN1 ==10 & df$CN2 ==10 & df$CL
==28 ,] ,
```

```
aes ( x = BL1 , y = P_ES , color = factor ( BL2 ) ) ) + geom
_ line ()
9 ggsave ('result .png ',g )
```

Figures 2-9 through 2-12 depict some examples of these graphs.

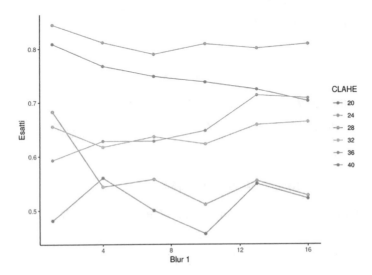

Figure 2-9. *CLAHE and BLUR 1. The value CLAHE = 24 gives positive results regardless of the variation of the BLUR 1 parameter*

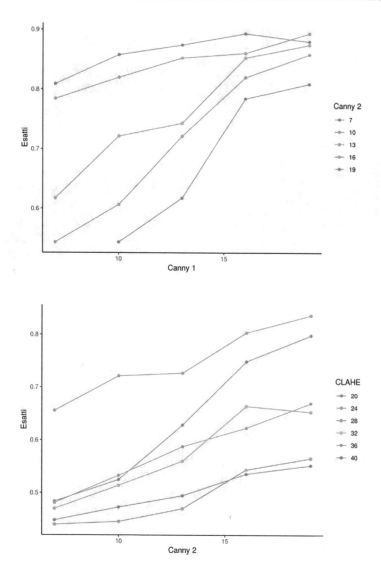

Figure 2-10. *CLAHE and CANNY 2. Another example where the value CLAHE = 24 gives better results than the others, but CANNY 2 returns positive results with higher values*

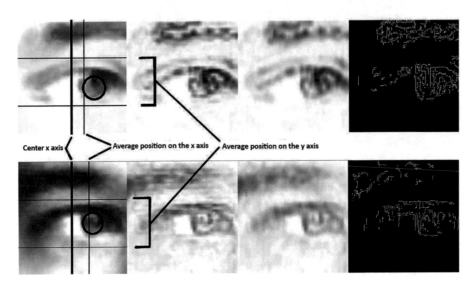

Figure 2-11. *CLAHE and BLUR 1. BLUR 1 gives better results with lower values*

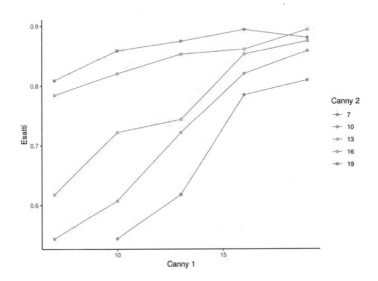

Figure 2-12. *CANNY 1 and CANNY 2. In this example, the relationship between CANNY 1 and 2 is highlighted, confirming that CANNY 2 has better performance with higher values (20)*

Analysis

After an analysis of the graphs that were generated by the script in R, it was possible to establish optimal ranges for each parameter. In order to make optimal recognition of the iris and establish the direction, the values used for the analysis were:

    CANNY 1 = 16
    CANNY 2 = 10
    BLUR1=1BLUR 2 = 16
    CLAHE = 24

Iris Recognition (2)

The objective here is to geometrically recognize the position of the iris, after having applied the photographic effects illustrated in the previous algorithms.

Modeling and Development

Once the optimal values for each parameter are chosen (described in the "Parameter Analysis" section), iris recognition has been implemented on the final effect of the CANNY. It was much easier to establish what the contours of the eye really were, in particular the iris and sclera.

To obtain the average of the last positions of the iris, a new one was created and the data structure containing the history of the last "n" acknowledgments on the axes x and y was used. This structure is saved in the multidimensional matrix, already containing the eye data, since the iris recognition is strictly linked to a particular eye (see Figure 2-13).

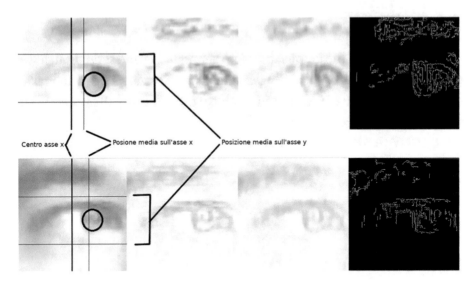

Figure 2-13. *Screenshot of the iris recognition*

Conclusions and Problems

Based on the approximate data on the position of the iris, it was possible
to detect an approximate recognition of the direction of the gaze (left,
right, center). The procedure was to consider half of the axis x (the
horizontal center of the image) and add or remove an offset prefixed (for
example, 30px).

The results were not very satisfactory: the eye was not perfectly
centered as OpenCV functions are not very precise in detecting the
position. Furthermore, the previously entered data structure has as a
consequence an approximation of the position. It's useful for eliminating
false positives, but the recognition of the eye can slightly decentralize if the
subject makes movements.

As a consequence, establishing the direction based on factors
related to the size and center of the image has led to the generation of
geometric errors.

An example of an error is evident in Figure 2-14: it can be seen that, despite the subject looking to the left, the algorithm recognizes (erroneously) that the gaze is directed toward the center or slightly to right.

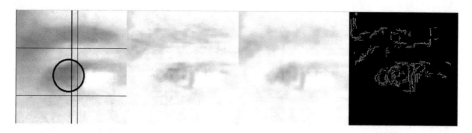

Figure 2-14. *Screenshot of the iris recognition*

"Average Color" Recognition

The objective here is to recognize the direction (center, right, or left) based on the color average of a dynamically selected area.

Modeling and Development

The results of the recognition of the iris, described in the previous section, were not the desired ones. Therefore, I focused my attention on color. I modified the algorithm to provide the average of the color in defined areas calculated based on the average of the last positions of the iris (using the data produced by the algorithm described in the "Recognition of the Iris" section).

In particular, two squares are designated to the right and left of a certain position. The y axis of this position is given by the mean position of the iris in the last frames. For the x axis, on the other hand, the position is calculated as a percentage of the recognized eye width.

In Figure 2-15, it is possible to see the two squares calculated as described. The lines, vertical and horizontal, represent the average position of the iris on the y and x axes, respectively. The circle represents the iris recognized in the last frame.

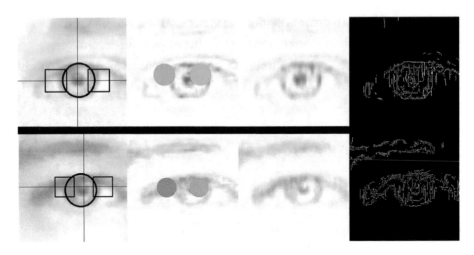

Figure 2-15. *Screenshot of the iris recognition*

Once the quadratic areas were designated, it was possible to calculate the mean of the color inside them, as shown in Figure 2-16.

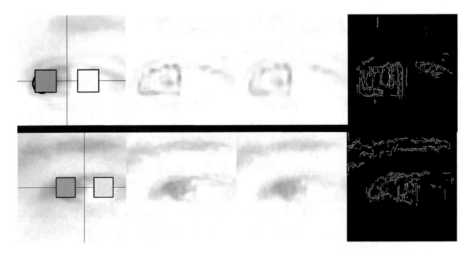

Figure 2-16. *Screenshot of the iris recognition*

It can be noted that the mean of the left rectangle is considerably more dark than the mean of the rectangle on the right. This happens since being the direction of gaze to the left, the iris covers the area of the rectangle left, making the "medium color" darker.

Therefore, the direction of the gaze can be established by subtracting the values of the respective areas. Obviously, the result obtained will be between -255 and 255 (maximum color values expressed in hexadecimal). A value far from 0 (for example -80) will indicate that the gaze is directed on the one hand, vice versa having values close to 0 (for example 13), when the look is facing the center. Specifically, negative values indicate a left direction while the positives indicate right.

Conclusions

Based on the approximate data on the position of the iris, it was possible to detect an approximate recognition of the direction of the gaze (left, right, center). The procedure was to consider half of the axis x (the horizontal center of the image) and add or remove an offset prefixed (for example, 30px).

The results were not very satisfactory. The eye was not perfectly centered as OpenCV functions are not very precise in detecting the position, furthermore the previously entered data structure has as a consequence an approximation of the position. This is useful for eliminating false positive, but it can slightly decentralize the recognition of the eye if the subject moves.

As a consequence, establishing the direction based on factors related to the size and center of the image has led to the generation of geometric errors.

Project Analysis

Data Analysis

In order to evaluate the efficiency of the algorithm, the following metrics were used: Precision, Recall, and F-measure. These three metrics are closely related. The measurement terms used are effective direction (the direction of the actual gaze of the subject), Eye 1, and Eye 2 (the direction recognized by the algorithm for each eye present), all evaluated on the number of total frames.

Precision

Precision measures, relative to the data, the ratio of true positives (number of times the direction was found correctly) and the sum between true positives and false positives (number of times the direction was detected incorrectly).

$$\textbf{Precision} = \frac{\textbf{n true positives}}{\textbf{Positives} + \textbf{n false positives}}$$

Recall

Recall measures, in relation to the data, the relationship between the true positives and the sum of various positives and false negatives (direction of the eye not recognized).

$$\textbf{Precision} = \frac{\textbf{n true positives}}{\textbf{N true Positives} + \textbf{n false positives}}$$

F-measure

The F-measure represents the relationship between the two previous metrics just described.

$$F\text{-}measure = \frac{n\ negative\ positives}{N\ true\ Positives + n\ false\ negatives}$$

All the results of the previous formulas are between 0 and 1 and are considered better the closer they get to the value 1.

Result

These metrics were used in particular for five videos, with different subjects, calculating for each one:

- Total number of frames.

- Number of frames in which the subject looks to the center

- Number of frames in which the subject looks to the right

- Number of frames in which the subject looks to the left

Once this data has been obtained, the algorithm has been appropriately modified for each of the videos, so that you can calculate the successes and failures management recognition. The data is then converted to a CSV file to be easily analyzed with spreadsheets.

Figures 2-17 through 2-24 show the expected results of Video #1, Video #2, Video #3, and Video #4 based on the Precision values. The precision measures, relative to the data, the ratio of true positives (number of times the direction was found correctly) and the sum between true positives and false positives (number of times the direction was detected incorrectly).

In Video #1, we see the detection expected based on Eye 1 and Eye 2.

Video #1

Direction Expected

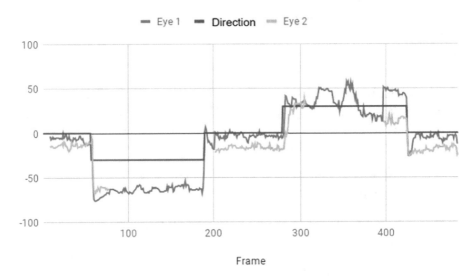

Figure 2-17.   *Video data for video #1*

Precision	Recall	F-measure
	0,88	0,89

In Video #1, we see the detection expected based on Eye 1 and Eye 2 shown in the real example (see Figure 2-18).

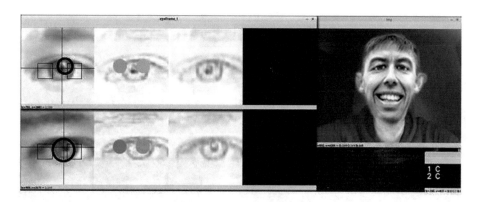

Figure 2-18. *Application screenshot (video 1)*

In Video #2, we see the detection expected based on Eye 1 and Eye 2 (see Figure 2-19).

Video #2

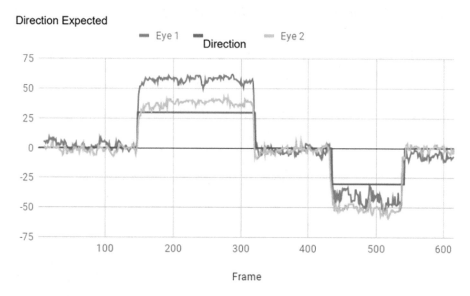

Figure 2-19. *Video data 2*

Precision	Recall	F-measure
	0,97	0,98

In Video #2, we see the detection expected based on Eye 1 and Eye 2, shown in the real example (see Figure 2-20).

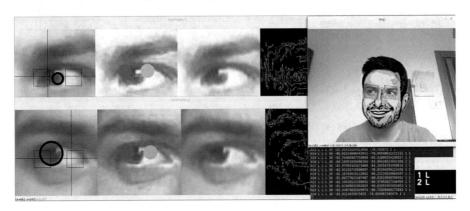

Figure 2-20. *Application screenshot (video 2)*

In Video #3, we see the detection expected based on Eye 1 and Eye 2 (see Figure 2-21).

Video #3

Direction Expected

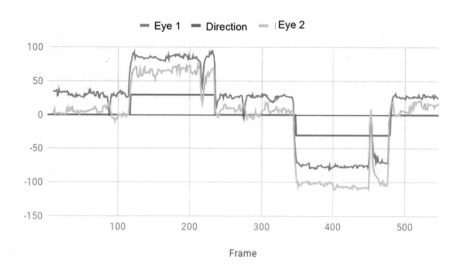

Figure 2-21. *Video data for video #3*

Precision	Recall	F-measure
	0,79	0,8

In Video #3, we see the detection expected based on Eye 1 and Eye 2 shown in the real example (see Figure 2-22).

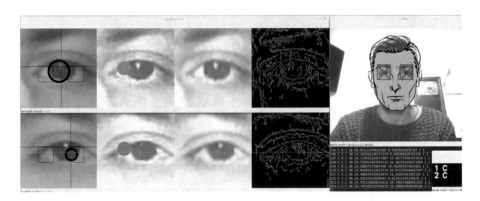

Figure 2-22. *Application screenshot (video 3)*

In Video #4, we see the detection expected based on Eye 1 and Eye 2 (see Figure 2-23).

Video #4

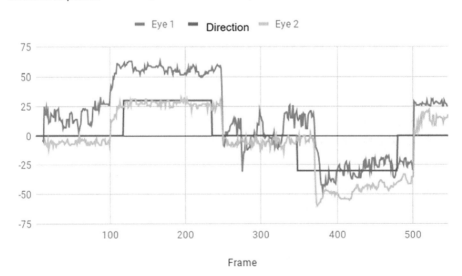

Figure 2-23. *Video data 4*

Precision	Recall	F-measure
	0,75	0,74

In Video #4, we see the detection expected based on Eye 1 and Eye 2 shown in the real example (see Figure 2-24).

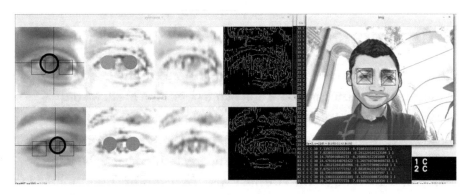

Figure 2-24. *Application screenshot (video 4)*

Summary Table

	N Frame	Eye 1	Eye 2	Precision	Recall	F-measure
Video #1	484	430	216	0,76	0,74	0,75
Video #2	616	473	466	0,99	0,97	0,98
Video #3	547	384	464	0,80	0,79	0,80
Video #4	546	362	344	0,76	0,74	0,75

The summary table highlights the relative results, summarized to videos. As you can see, Precision, Recall, and F-measure are always above 75% in all the videos, demonstrating that the algorithm has good effectiveness. The results may vary because, as mentioned, external factors (exposure, brightness, etc.) can affect recognition. Despite these variations, the effectiveness achieved is very high.

Project Conclusions

The object of this study was the search for a more effective algorithm possible in recognizing the direction of the gaze. First of all, we did research on existing software in order to evaluate whether there were eye-tracking algorithms with commonly used cameras, such as those of smartphones. This reflection is important precisely because the purpose is not to use dedicated hardware but to use the algorithm by exploiting the devices already widespread.

Noting the absence of effective algorithms, the work was oriented precisely to the creation of this algorithm: the set goal was therefore the identification of the direction of the gaze in an approximate way.

Several algorithms were created and evaluated for effectiveness and efficiency. The various paths they followed were partly progressive and partly parallel: For some tests, it was possible to identify positive aspects which could be useful and other negative aspects that made the effectiveness of the algorithm unsatisfactory with respect to the set objectives. Some tests were carried out in parallel as they involved different paths. In the light of the various tests, a final algorithm has been defined which reflects the initial requirements.

Consequently, with respect to the set objectives, the results can be deemed achieved. The Precision, Recall, and F-measure, as shown in the previous chapter, are sufficiently high. Furthermore, the choice of the Python language and the OpenCV framework allow for considerable portability, allowing the algorithm to be exported to various platforms and operating systems, such as Android.

Summary

This chapter focused on HCI design in video game user interfaces to suit the game's human-computer interaction functions. Eye-tracking tools were also found to be useful in the creation of online apps. The gaming industry, in particular, employs these strategies in the production of effective games. We'll further concentrate on video game creation utilizing HCI approaches in the next two chapters.

CHAPTER 3

Developing a Video Game

Anyone who has ever picked up a joystick, smartphone, or a remote control knows that a video game is in fact a point of contact between the gamers and their imaginations.

Video games possess boundless powers: they can show the players alternate universes, allow them to experience ordinary situations as extraordinary characters, and offer the possibility to visit worlds whose only limit is the imagination.

This chapter analyzes the process and various facets of game development. In tandem with the knowledge you'll acquire in the next chapter, you'll be able to tackle the development of a video game yourself using a programming language like Python.

In particular, this chapter explores the following points:

- Understanding the game industry's main stakeholders: the publisher, producer, and game developer.

- Reviewing game development in detail, analyzing the different processes into which it is divided: game design, game art design, game programming, and game testing. The developer roles needed for each of these facets are also described in detail.

J. T. George and M. J. George, *Human-Computer Interaction in Game Development with Python*, https://doi.org/10.1007/978-1-4842-8182-6_3

- Introducing and transitioning to the next chapter, which deals with software development and gaming software, by introducing two of the most popular models of agile development: Scrum and Personal Software Process.

- Explaining the stages of game development ranging from design of a new video game in the pre-production phase through its actual release at the beginning of the post-production phase.

- Providing a short but important explanation of one of the most discussed processes in the industry—*localization*. This is the linguistic and contextual adaptation of a product with respect to the needs of the country in which you want to market it.

Roles in the Video Game Industry

In this section, we review the tasks and analyze the working relationships between the three main players of the gaming industry.

Producers

"Producers basically manage the relationship with the artist. They find the talent, work out product deals, get contracts signed, manage them, and bring them to their conclusion. The producers do most of the things that a product manager does. They don't do the marketing, which in some cases product managers do. They don't make decisions about packaging and merchandising, but they do get involved ... they're a little life book editors, a little bit like film producers, and a lot like product managers"[1].

Trip Hawkins,
Founder of Electronic Arts

Although today the term is an industry standard, over the course of time, the role of *producer* has had various definitions. In principle, it is possible to frame the producer as the person responsible for supervising the development of a video game. Producers can be classified as external or internal.

Externals are usually employed by the game publisher and can act as executive producers, informing the publisher of the status of projects, managing the company's products, and making sure the game meets its time and budget goals. *Internals*, on the other hand, work for the developer and have an active role in development. Generally, those who cover the latter role will have to negotiate contracts and license agreements, manage programs and budget, supervise artistic and technical development, ensure the delivery of the final product within the stable time limits, arrange beta tests and localizations, and submit ideas to editors.

For the most part, the producers do not play a hands-on role in the actual design of the game, though they wield some influence over its development, because they have to reconcile the wishes of the publisher with those of the developer (see Figure 3-1).

---

[1]https://www.hmoob.in/wiki/Game_director

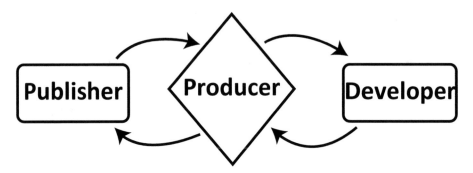

Figure 3-1. *The producer represents the contact element between the publisher and the developer*

Publishers

A publisher is a firm that releases video games created by an outside studio or studios. Big firms distribute their own titles, while smaller organizations rely on third-party distributors. The publisher is responsible for deciding on and perhaps paying for the game's licensing, as well as covering expenses related to localization, packaging, and possible manuals. Because the publisher typically funds a game's development, it tries to mitigate risk by employing a team of producers or project managers to keep track on the developer's work.

Most video games made by an outside developer are paid on a regular basis when specified development milestones are met. In recent years, the game industry has shifted to a hit-driven paradigm, as a result of customers' continued purchase of mass market titles, causing lesser productions to suffer and finding themselves with less and less market space.

Every publisher has begun to devote increasingly large expenditures to development in order to make their games the best of their genre, pressuring internal teams to focus on popular franchise sequels rather than exploring new intellectual properties. Companies like Activision Blizzard, and Electronic Arts, for example, have bought several talent teams with unique ideas and then assigned them supporting roles in other series, resulting in countless critiques.

Game Developers

A *game developer* is a software developer who focuses on video game development. A game developer can be a single individual or a major corporation with programmers, designers, and artists on staff. A developer can focus on a single console, such as the Nintendo Switch, Xbox One, or PlayStation 4, or create projects for many platforms. Other developers concentrate on game porting from one platform to another or on game location. There are several categories of game developers:

- A *first-party developer* is part of a company that manufactures and sells a game console and develops titles exclusively for it. Such a developer may use the company name, such as Sony Interactive Entertainment, have a specific division name, such as Sony Santa Monica or Team Ico, or may have been an independent studio before being acquired by the console manufacturer, such as Naughty Dog or Insomniac Games. Using first-party developers allows console makers to avoid paying royalties on game profits.

- A *second-party developer* is a studio that makes deals with a console manufacturer, agreeing to produce video games exclusively for it. In exchange for this exclusivity, manufacturers offer higher royalty payments than to those required by third-party developers. These studios maintain their independence and are therefore free, at the end of the contract, to continue developing games for themselves or others. Some examples of second-party companies are Remedy Entertainment and Game Freak.

- A *third-party developer* can work for a publisher or develop and publish games independently. In the first case, the publisher and developer sign a contract that specifies a series of milestones that must be met within a certain period of time. The publisher can check the status of the work at any time to make sure that deadlines are met or to direct the developer if the game does not meet expectations. Upon achieving each milestone, the publisher pays the developer an advance against royalties. Larger third-party development studios sometimes maintain multiple development teams, so that they can work with multiple publishers simultaneously. However, third-party developers tend to be comprised of a small team. Third-party game development is an unstable, risky endeavor, as small developers can become totally dependent on a single publisher's revenue and a canceled game can lead to the studio's collapse. In recent years, large publishers have acquired numerous third-party studios, allowing them to maintain their own culture and their own work practices, in exchange for exclusive products and financial control.

  Activision, for example, has acquired numerous studios, such as infinity Ward, Treyarch, and Vicarious Visions. Publishers tend to have more understanding attitudes toward their teams when they find themselves over budget or miss deadlines, compared to third-party developers (see Figure 3-2).

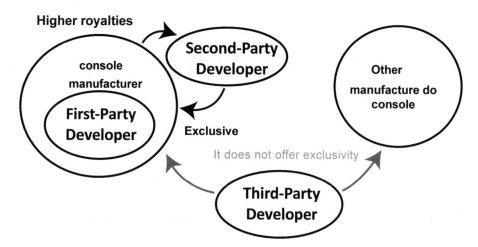

Figure 3-2. *Relationships between developers and console manufacturers*

Roles and Processes of Game Development

As mentioned in the previous section, video game development covers multiple sectors and therefore different professional roles are required to complete a development team. Such a team can be composed of a small number of developers, as is the case with some independent studies, up to groups of hundreds of people. What doesn't vary are the roles that team members can hire within the sector. A development team includes the roles described in the following paragraphs (see Figure 3-3).

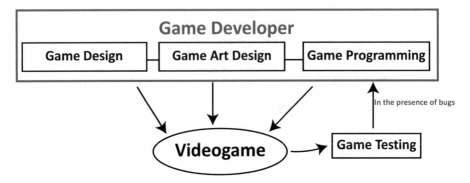

Figure 3-3. *Relationship between the various processes of game development*

Game Design

Game design is the pre-production process of creating the framework and rules for video games, as well as the gameplay design, story, and characters in the production phase. Game designers are in charge of this process. As a result, their responsibility is to define a title's gameplay, i.e., how it works, how playable it is, and how enjoyable it is to play. As artists, architects, entertainers, and educators, game designers can be thought of as artists, architects, entertainers, educators, and even gods, because every character and player will have to obey the plot and rules that they developed.

- The *lead designer* occupies a similar role to that occupied by the director of a film, in addition to giving birth to the idea of the video game, this person coordinates the work of other designers, ensures communication between teams, makes design decisions, and presents the game on the outside. The more difficult is task to have an original basic idea and at the same captivating time and to present innovative gameplay solutions and fun. Often a lead designer is also a great writer and takes on the task of defining the entire plot of the video game as a real script. The designer usually produces an initial proposal, containing among other things the concept, the gameplay, the list of features, the target to which the game is addressed, system requirements, and programs to use and estimates of budget. The designer then fine-tunes everything during development.

In reality, due to lack of funding, few games are truly guided by the ideas of the designer and are therefore forced to follow the market. In fact, it is not uncommon for a publisher to come under pressure on a lead designer to push them to change some aspects or simply to change the release date of the title by doing it coincide with strategic dates within the gaming market. Often these decisions have led to the release of incomplete video games that are full of bugs, as in the case of *Assassin's Creed – Unity* or in the worst case, of actual failures.

"Here are a lot more choices possible. Think of the script as a complex film like *Pulp Fiction* resides on 160 pages, while it Detroit script took over 3,000 pages"[2]

—Adam Williams, Lead Writer for *Detroit: Become Human*

- The *level designer* has the task of creating the levels and the different environments of the video and of enriching the experience with unique challenges and various missions. Designers often find themselves

---

[2] https://gaming.hwupgrade.it/articoli/videogames/5154/detroit-per-ps4-molto-piu-di-un-film-interattivo_index.html

working with incomplete versions of the product, with prototypes and placeholders, aiming to obtain clean consistency and layout before the graphics are completed. Level design is required to provide players a goal to reach and offer them the same pleasant experience. Sometimes level designers create hidden rooms or secret levels that, in exchange for additional rewards, require greater effort on the part of the player. It is also not uncommon to find so-called Easter eggs, containing messages such as names or images of the designers themselves or funny quotes or references to other works (see Figure 3-4).

Figure 3-4. *An open-source level editor provided by Sony*

Figure 3-5. *Celeste, one of the best Pixel Art video games*

Game Art Design

Game art design is the process of creating the artistic aspects of a video game. This process begins during the pre-production phase, in which the visual artists, or alternatively the designers themselves, make rough sketches of characters, environments, and objects. In the later stages, the *art programmers* are completed and brought to life through graphic design. *Artworks* have a significant impact on development and sales of a game, as many customers use graphics as a yardstick for the validity of a title. In the early days of game development, the figure of the game artist coincided with that of the programmer, because these old games had minimalist graphics. From the first in the 1980s, art design began to occupy an ever-greater space in the development of a video game, up to three dimensions a mid-90s. Today, many art designers create realistic graphics by modeling characters on real actors and using film sets as a background, while others continue to use minimal graphics or graphics composed in *pixel* art (see Figure 3-6).

- *The art director* monitors the results of other art designers and ensures that these results interact coherently with each other. They often works with other game development figures and get involved up at the end of development.

- The *concept artist* produces sketches of characters, environments, and storyboards following the vision of the artistic director. The *concept art* produced is then used as a demonstration and then resumed in the following stages.

- The *storyboard artist* develops the game footage and creates an outline to follow for the rest of the art designers, for the programmers, and the writers.

- The *2D artist* creates and adds *textures* to the 3D models thus giving depth to video games, creates the *sprites* of characters and objects, deals with static assets for the creation of levels and maps, and works with the *interface programmer* to produce game interfaces as a menu and HUD3.

- The *3D modeler* uses digital software, such as Maya, 3DS Studio Max, and Blender, to make characters, weapons, vehicles, or buildings. The artist specializing in the construction of game worlds, layouts, and landscapes is called *environmental designer.*

- The *lighting artist* works on the dynamics of the lights, adjusting colors and brightness to add different emotions to the game. The goal of this artist is to create an atmosphere suitable for the scenes.

- The animator takes care of giving life to the characters, the environment, and everything that moves in a video game.

Game Programming

Game programming is the development and programming process of the game code. A newly developed video game might include advanced physics, artificial intelligence, digitized and complex sound strategies, and different input devices, and be playable over the Internet or over a LAN. Every aspect mentioned, given its complexity, can take a long time. For this reason every programmer specializes in a different area.

- *Game engine programmers* take care of the engine development game, which includes physics and simulated graphics. Video games, due to the high cost of a proprietary engine, often use existing, free, or open engines sources.

- The *physics engine programmer* is dedicated to the development of the physics used in the game. They generally only simulate some aspects of real physics and, given the high computational cost, shortcuts are use. They only give the impression that the physical phenomena present are faithful to reality. In other cases, however, to allow for simpler gameplay or effects theatrical, the physics is altered. With the development of graphics and content, the movements of the characters are no longer managed by the programmers, but adjusted via *motion capture*.

- The title of *graphic engine programmer* in the past belonged to a programmer who dealt with optimizations of 2D graphics and the development of blitter algorithms, i.e., combinations of bitmaps through a Boolean function. However, today it comes exclusively applied to programmers specialized in development and modification of complex 3D graphic renderings. This requires a solid knowledge of advanced mathematical concepts such as vector mathematics and linear algebra. The programmers collaborate closely with technical artists and must also be familiar with shader programming.

- An *artificial intelligence programmer* handles one of the more important and difficult tasks among those present. In fact, this person deals with stimulating the intelligence of each non-player character by programming attack strategies, paths, actions, and reactions. The main purpose is to make them as similar as possible to those controlled by the player, increasing their unpredictability and ability. Some strategy games, such as those from the *Civilization* series, or games role-playing like *The Elder Scrolls,* heavily use artificial intelligence , while others, such as *puzzle games,* exploit it with thrift.

- *Sound programmers* are in charge of creating and managing scripting that will then be used by the sound designers. These tools allow the association of sounds to characters, actions, objects, and events and the assignment of atmospheric sounds to game environments. They develop environmental variables such as reverberation and echoes.

- *Gameplay programmers* focus on implementing the mechanics and logic of the video game. Initially, all events were part of the main code written by gameplay programmers. However, today, the game engine takes care of rendering graphics, sound, and physics while remaining separate from programming. On the contrary, scripts deal with, through scripting languages, program events, non-player character behaviors, and objectives.

- At smaller companies, there is no distinction between game programmers based on these jobs, and programmers wind up working in several positions.

- *UI programmers* specialize in programming user interfaces and usually develop additional usable libraries. They often use the same 3D technology as the rest of the game and special effects such as transparency, animations, and particle effects.

Figure 3-6. *PlayStation Move, a motion-sensitive controller*

- *The input programmer* is responsible for managing the influence of input devices on the game, such as keyboards, mice, and joysticks. More and more advanced devices have been introduced, such as the Wii controller and the PlayStation Move (see Figure 3-6), which means that this process is much more complex.

- *The network programmer* takes care of the code that allows players to cooperate or compete on the Internet or a LAN. Network latency, packet compression, and broken connections are some of the main challenges that these programmers are faced with.

- *The game tools programmer* takes care of creating custom tools in order to compile scripts, import or convert artistic assets, and edit layers in real time. Such tools have specific functions for a given game. For example, an adventure game developer might need one editor for dialog boxes, while a sports game developer could use an editor to manage player and team statistics.

- *Porting programmers* are in charge of converting game code from one operating system to another. Porting can often involve the total rewriting of the code, as proprietary languages or older tools make conversion complicated and inefficient.

- *The lead game programmer* is responsible for all programming of the game and makes sure that the various submodules are implemented correctly. This person also has to attend many meetings.

Game Testing

Game testing is the quality control process for video games. These tests require computer skills, analytics, and skills of critical evaluation and resistance, with the aim of discovering and documenting all software defects. A typical game testing sequence is the following:

1. Incorrect game behavior is identified and analyzed.

2. The bug is reported to developers through a specific tracking system by attaching real-time video or reports.

3. The developer responsible for the bug checks for the bug.

4. The test, after the changes made by the developer, checks if the error has been resolved.

Some bugs can be claimed as a feature of the game, defined as not a bug, or are ignored with the permission of the publisher or the designers.

Software Development

Generally, the software lifecycle is based on the *waterfall model,* which structures the software development process in a linear sequence, including requirements analysis, design, testing, and maintenance. Despite the video game being software, this model it is not suitable for its development, and it is therefore necessary to search for a different method. What suits video games best is *agile development,* based on *software prototyping*, a cyclical process of prototyping, testing, analysis, and product refinement. In this way, the interaction with the designed system is used as a form of research to obtain feedback and refine the different iterations of the game by gradually adding increasing feature sets. Some of the most popular methods of agile development are described in this section.

Scrum: A lightweight, iterative, and incremental framework for the management of complex jobs, such as software development. The term comes from the scrums found in rugby and was chosen to emphasize teamwork. It is based on three fundamental pillars:

- **Transparency.** Significant aspects of the development process must be visible to those responsible for the work and they must be defined by a common standard in such a way that observers share the same understanding of what is to come.

- **Inspection.** Qualified inspectors must frequently check the artifacts produced and the progress made to achieve the pre-established goals.

- **Adaptation.** If some aspects of the development process go over acceptable limits, inspectors must take action on the process itself or on the material produced to minimize the deviation from the pre-established objectives.

Scrum divides the work into a series of compatible objectives in timed iterations, called *sprints*, each made up of multiple phases. A *sprint planning meeting* is held at the beginning of each cycle in which the work to be carried out in the corresponding sprint and the *sprint backlog* is prepared, containing details on the time needed to achieve each goal. Later, a project team meeting is held in the same place and at the same time, for 15 minutes, in which each team member explains what was done in the last meeting, what will be done after the current one, and which obstacles have been encountered, which will be documented by the scrum master to be solved. More time is dedicated to the *product backlog grooming*, the process of reviewing backlog articles, in which they are properly prepared and sorted to make them clear and executable for teams. The scrum of scrums is then held, which allows different teams to discuss their work by paying particular attention to areas of overlap and integration.

The team's work after the last meeting is also reported, the work to be done before the next meeting, if there are any obstacles or slowdowns, and if the team achieved results that can be used by other teams. At the end of the sprint, two meetings are held—the sprint review, in which the *product backlog* is adapted and the increase is inspected, and the sprint retrospective, in which the team creates an improvement plan to be implemented. Scrum defines three roles to ensure optimal communication between the members of the team:

- The product owner represents stakeholder 1 and the voice of the customer. They define the product requirements centered on needs of the buyer, give them priority, and add them to the product backlog.

- The development team is responsible for the delivery of the product, making it potentially releasable at the end of each sprint. It is made up of less than ten self-organized and committed members in analysis, design, development, testing, and in the documentation.

- The *scrum master* is responsible for removing obstacles that limit the team's ability to achieve the goal of the sprint. They hold enforcement authority, chair important meetings, and are ultimately called upon to keep the team focused on work, eliminating outside influences.

Personal Software Process (PSP): Created by Watts Humphrey, this process aims at providing software engineers with disciplined methods to improve their software development processes and their analytical skills, making only commitments that they can maintain, managing the quality of their designs, and reducing the number of defects. PSP is based on a series of levels, each of which has detailed scripts, checklists, and templates to guide the developer through fundamental steps of development. The process involves the following steps:

- PSP0 has three phases—planning, development and postmortem—where you need to make sure that all data has been correctly recorded and analyzed.

- PSP0.1 adds a coding standard and the development of an improvement plan to record new ideas.

- PSP1, based on the data collected previously, estimates the size of the project and reports the test results.

- PSP 1.1 uses data and determines the time it takes to plan activities and schedules.

- PSP 2 focuses on reviewing the design and code, removing bugs and flaws.

- PSP 2.1 introduces design specifications and analysis techniques.

One of the main aspects of the PSP is the use of data to analyze and improve performance, the collection of which is based on the following elements. The scripts provide guidance for the various stages of the process and suggestions for applying the measures. Measures are identified in size that estimate part of the product, such as lines of code. Effort is the time it takes to complete an activity. Quality is the number of product defects and, finally, a measure of the progress plotted against the planned dates.

Finally, there are the standards that guarantee accuracy and data consistency. The PSP's goal is the production of high-quality software, i.e. software with a low number of defects that meets the users' needs. The structure of the phases allows developers to detect defects early. The PSP theory is that it is cheaper and more effective to remove defects as close as possible to where and when they were inserted, so developers are encouraged to conduct continuous design and code reviews.

We've seen how the various jobs in the software development cycle are handled. We will now concentrate on the actual game development phase. This is critical knowledge for anyone starting from scratch in game production.

Game Development Phases

Pre-Production Phase

The pre-production phase is a planning phase focused on developing ideas and concepts and producing clear and understandable documentation describing all tasks, schedules, and estimates for the development team. A so-called suite of documents is formed for the production plan. The documents produced in this phase are, in order of compilation, the following:

- *The high concept,* which is a brief description of the game in which you try to answer the question "what is the game about?"

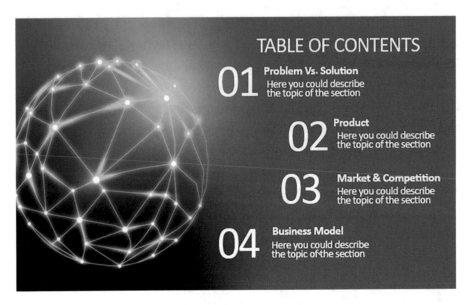

TABLE OF CONTENTS

01 **Problem Vs. Solution**
Here you could describe
the topic of the section

02 **Product**
Here you could describe
the topic of the section

03 **Market & Competition**
Here you could describe
the topic of the section

04 **Business Model**
Here you could describe
the topic of the section

Figure 3-7. *An example of a pitch page*

- The *pitch*, a short document created with the aim of
  presenting the strengths of the game and justifying its
  development at an economic level. Before obtaining
  consent, the developers of a game may have to meet
  with several publisher executives and, in some cases,
  present a playable demo (see Figure 3-7).

- The *concept*, which is a much more detailed document
  and includes all information produced about the game,
  including the high concept, the genre, the description
  of the gameplay, the plot, the target audience, the
  hardware platforms, the team requirements, and the
  marketing analysis risk. Before a project is approved,
  a group of artists realizes the concept art of the game
  resources, while some programmers start developing
  quick-and dirty prototypes with the purpose of showing
  some features of the game. During this phase, the

producers are engaged in planning the program, budget, and tasks in order to create a solid production plan and avoid initial delays.

- The *game design document*, which is a document produced at the beginning of large-scale production and incorporates most of the starting material. This document describes in detail the concept of the game, the main elements, and may include preliminary sketches of the various aspects. This document stays alive for the duration of the development cycle and is modified daily or weekly. Often accompanying it are game prototypes that allow developers to experiment with different algorithms and scenarios.

The prototyping during the pre-production phase is carried out on paper because it makes it easier to test and make changes, preventing the waste of time and resources. A successful development model is iterative prototyping, where the design is refined based on the progress achieved during each iteration.

Outsourcing

Several disciplines, such as audio, dubbing, and motion capture, are present for a short period of the development cycle, but they require intensive time and costs. For this reason, small- and medium-sized companies often outsource these skills, using third-party teams to create them. Outsourcing plans are filled in precisely during the pre-production phase. Among the most influenced disciplines, dubbing is often outsourced, as it requires a lot of specialized skills, sound effects production, and music. The cost varies according to the length of the composition, the method of execution, and the composer's experience.

Production Phase

The production stage is the main stage of development, when teams develop the game asset products and source codes. It's the moment in which all the staff are actively involved in the production of the game: programmers program new code, composers compose music, writers write dialogue, artists develop graphics, etc.

Game design is a necessary process for creating the content and regulations of a video game, and it necessitates aesthetic, technical, and literary abilities. During the production phase, designers implement and change the design to suit the game's current concept. Features and layers are frequently deleted or added, the graphic style evolves, and the target audience and platform may shift. All of these modifications should be indicated on the design document.

- During this phase, programmers continuously develop prototypes to test ideas, many of which may never make it to the final product. They incorporate new features required by designers and fix any bugs. Even using a standard game engine, you need intensive programming to customize the different aspects of your game.

- Creating layers is included in this phase. Paradoxically, the first level of the game is the one that takes the most time to develop. This is because the tools for creation continually require new features that will be used to develop the next layers. Such features could make previous layers obsolete by forcing developers to update them. In addition, the next levels can be developed much faster since the set of features is more complete and the vision of the game is clearer and more stable.

- *Audio production* can be divided into three categories: sound effects, music, and dubbing. The production of sound effects consists of the production of new sounds by modifying a sample with particular effects or replicating it with real instruments. Music, on the other hand, can be synthesized or performed live and there are several ways in which it is presented in a game. Music can be ambient and be used to strengthen the aesthetic mood and game environment; it can be triggered by events, as happens *in Super Mario Bros.;* it can indicate action, such as music composed of frenetic and rapidly changing soundtracks; or it can accompany game menus.

- Toward the end of the production phase, when everything is playable, the testers begin their work. Testing a game initially takes little time, and testers can work on multiple titles at once. However, the closer the development comes to the conclusion, the more a single game requires an increasing number of full-time testers. At this stage, features and levels have been completed quickly and there are numerous new features compared with the initial stages. Subtle changes to the code can lead to unexpected changes, so testers must approach each new feature and perform *regression tests,* the set of tests carried out on the previous functions of the game.

Milestones: The Cornerstones of Development

Milestones are used to track progress. The milestone list is based on the collaboration between the publisher and the developer. It represents, for the latter, the list of objectives to be achieved in order to obtain payment. A good publisher, with the guarantee that a milestone is completed, provides for the payment even if this turns out to be 90% of completion, since the developers have to bear monthly development expenses. In addition, the developer and publisher can find an agreement to reorganize the objectives to be achieved depending on the change in the resources. Generally, milestones are based on short descriptions of goals to be achieved, such as "Physics are working" or "Player roaming in game environment". However, milestones can also be based on the development cycle of the video game. The most common stages in a two-year cycle are as follows:

- The pre-alpha is the version containing representative assets and gameplay. It is the first version with functional gameplay elements and is often based on the prototype created during pre-production. The minor pre-alpha and alpha projects refer to the same phase, but large video games require pre-alpha. This phase occurs 12 to 18 months before the code is issued.

- An alpha-stage game is playable and contains all the main features, which will then be further reworked based on testing and feedback. At this stage, programmers focus on completing the code base rather than implementing new features. This phase occurs 8 to 10 months before the code is issued.

- Code freeze is the stage where no more code is added to the game and only bugs are fixed. It occurs three to four months before the code is released.

- The beta is the stage when the game is complete with features and resources. This version does not contain bugs that prevent the game from being submitted and does not require further code changes. It occurs two to three months before the code is released.

- Code release is the stage where many bugs have been fixed and the game is ready to be submitted for review by the console manufacturer. Such code is usually ready three weeks before release.

- A game in gold master is in the final version that will be used for production.

Post-Production Phase

The post-production phase is characterized by the continuous updating of the newly developed video game. In the past, titles released on consoles did not receive support or fixes until the release of a *port, sequel,* or *remake,* which used a lot of the game engine and previous resources. In more recent times, with the increasing spread of the Internet and online services such as *Xbox Game Pass,* Steam, and *PlayStation Network,* developers can continue to support their works for months or years, releasing patches and DLC1 downloadables for free or for a fee. PC development is influenced by the numerous possible hardware and software configurations that inevitably lead to errors not highlighted in the testing phase. For this reason, programmers allow players to send constant feedback and once they have obtained a sufficient number of reports to frame the problems, they begin the development of a corrective patch. Patch development can take weeks or months, as it is intended to fix most bugs and issues overlooked during the release stage or, in rare cases, fix those caused unintentionally by previous patches. Sometimes a patch can include extra features or content and, more rarely, change the gameplay itself. In the case of a massively multiplayer online game (MMOG), the release of the game coincides with the beginning of support, since such games are constantly being updated, updating that can be carried out by part of the original team or by an external team.

Localization

A game's localization is sometimes confused with a straightforward translation of the available language materials. In fact, the process encompasses all changes made to the video game, such as editing artistic assets, creating new packages and manuals, recording new audio, cutting entire sections of the game due to cultural differences, sensitivities, and/ or local legal requirements, and frequently even replacing deleted content with new content. Because the choice to *localize* a game is strongly influenced by economic reasons, such as the potential profits that may be generated in a new location, the job is usually done by the developers themselves or by a third-party team.

Furthermore, publishers frequently modify a game's graphic design and packaging to strengthen its connection with purchasers and adapt to local markets. The process of localization can be carried out at numerous levels:

- The first involves importing the game to another country in the original language, in order to reduce its costs.

- The second involves the localization of the entire documentation and packaging, but not the game itself. This strategy is used when the game has little text or a simple plot, or if the local buyer is expected to have a good command of the original language, as was the case with *Secret of Mana* in Sweden.

- The third involves a localization of only the game text, leaving the voiceovers in the original language. This strategy is used to reduce the costs required for hiring actors and for re-recording dialogue, while at the same time making the game understandable in another language.

- The fourth is based on a complete localization of the work. All assets are translated, including voiceovers, game text, graphics, and manuals. This option, due to its high cost, is usually undertaken only by the largest development companies.

Fan Translation

The advent of console emulation in the late 90s led to the emergence of communities of players interested in reproducing and modifying the titles they had played when they were young. The knowledge and tools that emerged from them, combined with the growing release of video games exclusively in Japanese, such as the *Final Fantasy and Dragon Quest* series, led to the creation of several communities of *fan translations*, which are unofficial translations of video games made by fans, with the aim of making these titles accessible to the Western market.

Fan translations can also be done to titles that received imperfect official localizations, as happened with *Bionic Commando*, to which several censorships were applied that led to the removal of content, or with *Phantasy Star*, in which the plot and names of the characters were changed. Over time, fan translations have been judged in different ways by copyright holders. In 2007, Koichiro Sakamoto, a producer at *Square Enix,* gave an interview in which he publicly thanked fans for their translations. However, on another occasion, *Square Enix* itself forced a hacker who had just completed a long-awaited translation of *Final Fantasy Type 0* to remove any reference to it, due to the simultaneous release of an HD version of the same title for PlayStation 4 and Xbox One. In 2010, publisher Xseed Games licensed *Ys: The Oath in Felghana* and requested a translation from fans for a fee in order to reduce localization costs.

The same year, *Rising Star Games* collaborated with Spanish fans to translate the Fragile Dreams script: *Farewell Ruins of The Moon.* At other times, publishers, noticing the great interest around a fan translation and the possible economic return, have created an official localization, as happened for *Trials of Mana.*

Summary

This chapter explained several roles of the gaming industry, including the roles of publisher, producer, and game developer. It discussed the steps of game creation, starting with the design of a new video game in the pre-production phase and ending with its release in the post-production phase.

In addition, this chapter contained a brief but crucial explanation of localization, which is the linguistic and contextual modification of a product to the demands of the region in which it is to be sold. The next chapter broadly traces the history of game development and highlights the turning points that have allowed the video game sector to grow exponentially and become so active and profitable.

CHAPTER 4

Turning Points in Game Development

This chapter broadly traces the history of game development and highlights the turning points that fueled the game industry's exponential growth into one of the most active and profitable in the world. It also introduces the main challenges faced by publishers, developers, and the industry as a whole. It covers the "crunch" phenomenon, which has increasingly become a point of concern to those working within the industry, as well as the ever-present threat of piracy. It provides the basic knowledge you'll need before proceeding to the next chapter and learning how to program a video game yourself. It also introduces the concepts of programming languages and programming paradigms, before exploring visual programming and the most used tools in game development: the game engine and game editor.

Game Engines

A *game engine* is a software development environment designed to allow the creation of video games on different platforms. Generally, it includes a rendering engine, an engine for simulating physics and detecting collisions, a timeline for animations, artificial intelligence, streaming, memory management, video support, and work scene. Game engines offer a flexible and extensible software platform containing all

J. T. George and M. J. George, *Human-Computer Interaction in Game Development with Python*, https://doi.org/10.1007/978-1-4842-8182-6_4

the basic functions, immediately ready to use, to develop a game while reducing costs, complexity, and time to market—the most critical factors in the video game industry. The main components of a game engine are discussed in the following sections.

Rendering Engine

The rendering engine is responsible for producing animated 3D visuals using one of numerous methods available, such as rasterization and ray tracing. They are often built on one or more rendering application programming interfaces, or APIs, such as Direct3D, OpenGL, or Vulkan, which offer software abstraction of the GPU.

Low-level libraries, such as DirectX, are also used because they provide access to the windowing system independent of the development platform and allow the program to assign a surface on a computer screen for graphics display (see Figure 4-1). Input devices, network adapters, and sound cards are also accessible through these libraries.

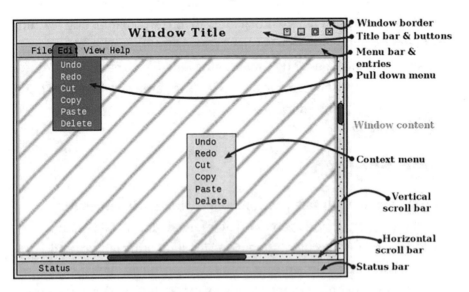

Figure 4-1. *Example of a windowing system, software that manages different parts of the screen separately*

- *Audio engine.* This component consists of algorithms related to loading, editing, and outputting sound. It must be able to load, decompress, and play audio files and, in the best of cases, simulate effects such as sound oscillation, echo, the Doppler effect, etc.

- *Physics engine.* This is responsible for the realistic simulation of the laws of physics within the video game and provides several functions to simulate physical forces and collisions by acting on objects at runtime.

- *AI (artificial intelligence).* This is present in an external module and must be designed by specialized software engineers. It's created for a certain type of game, as different video games implement different AIs.

Before the birth of game engines, developers designed video games as individual entities, often focusing on a certain console and being excessively limited by display management or low memory. The rapid development of hardware prevented the reuse of the same codes for which most projects followed a set of *hard-coded* rules, based on the use of a small number of layers and graphic data. During the golden age of arcade video games, it became common for video game companies to develop internal game engines for use with proprietary software. Some of these 2D creation systems were *Arcade Game Construction Kit, Wargame Construction Set,* and especially the ASCG Maker engines of *ASCII* and *Klik & Play.* The term "game engine" was born in the mid-90s in close contact with the continuous rise of 3D video games. The popularity of titles like *Doom* and *Quake* meant that many developers, instead of creating games from scratch, licensed the main components of the code, limiting themselves to producing the game assets. The abstraction of the hardware allowed the same game to run on different platforms with simple modifications of the source code, making the latter reusable even for the development of sequels or spin-offs. This marked a major turning point in the video game industry.

The improvement of the game engines led to an obvious separation between rendering, scripting, graphics, and level design, strongly influencing the composition of the development teams. Currently, game engines are developed on higher-level languages, such as Java and C#, and are used in sectors outside the video game sector, such as military, medical, and cinematographic areas.

Indie Video Games

An independent ("indie") video game is a title designed by small teams without the financial support of a large publisher and without a clear artistic control. Freedom in development allows independent developers to take risks not usually found in triple-A games, making indies known for innovation, creativity, and artistic experimentation. Team sizes can vary and external artists and musicians often contribute to the development as well. Many independent games have been created by a single developer, such as *Cave Story* and *Axiom Verge*.

The larger a team is, the higher the running costs, increasing the risk factor in the event of a failure. To fund the game, developers may rely on finding a publisher, starting a crowdfunding campaign, or building a community ready to support the game during development. The beginning of indie video game development is difficult to pinpoint, because, despite the fact that the first games were developed for mainframe computers in universities and other institutions without financial support, the video game industry did not foresee a commercial sector.

Generally, such works with PCs happened in the 70s when the domination of the market by consoles pushed programmers to self-distribute their games in stores or by mail order. In the 80s, shareware games became the main means of distributing demos, with which players had the opportunity to try the title before buying it in its full version. Such demos were generally free to distribute to developers and were often included in magazines, providing a hallmark for independent developers. In the mid-90s, the release of titles such as *Wolfenstein 3D* and *Doom* made the PC gaming platform able to compete with different consoles. This caused the disappearance of small independent teams, now unable to keep up with the costs, speed, and distribution of large commercial entities. Software technologies on the Internet along with the development of digital distribution that allowed you to sell directly to players, bypassing the costs and limits of retail distribution, led to the revival of indie games. The renewed interest in independent productions led game engine developers to offer their products cheaply, along with dedicated libraries and software, with the aim of supporting indie teams.

The appearance of digital stores such as Steam and GOG offered these developers the opportunity to publish and update their titles and players to download them at any time, while the store deals with managing sales and distributions. At the beginning of 2015, the perception was born, called *indiepocalypse,* that the rise of the independent market and the large number of easy-to-use tools for the creation of video games would lead to an excess of video game supply, saturating the market. Although the collapse did not occur, the independent market is now too large and only very few titles manage to get wide media coverage, the so-called *indie darlings*. These titles are identified through the reactions of consumers who buy and review the game positively. Among them are *Celeste* and *Untitled Goose Game,* winner of the "Game of the Year" award at the GDC Awards and the D.I.C.E. Awards.

Figure 4-2. *Pillars of Eternity, example of RPG with isometric view of game*

Crowdfunding

Crowdfunding is a phenomenon born in Australia and the United States, through which the promoter of an initiative requests, through a website, sums of money from the public with the aim of supporting their project. As for the gaming industry, this type of funding, as well as a means of making a game, is seen as a way for developers to determine the feedback from the public about their project, so as not to risk time and investment in a bad idea. Kickstarter in particular is a website in the United States created to provide financial support to creative projects and represents the most used crowdfunding platform in the video game, film, and music market.

On this platform, the creators of a project choose an expiration date and a minimum threshold of funds to be reached. If the latter is not reached by the deadline, the funds are not collected. Investors do not get a cash gain, but a material reward, such as a thank you letter or the product itself. Kickstarter does not claim any ownership rights over the projects produced, but those launched on the site are stored and accessible to the public permanently.

The Case of Dreams: Developing a Game Within a Video Game

Dreams is a sandbox video game developed by Media Molecule, creator of *The Little Big Planet* series. It offers the opportunity to face, in the role of a goblin, various levels of play, called dreams. However, *Dreams* possesses a fundamental characteristic that distinguishes it from the competition: the possibility of developing real video games. In *Dreams,* you can create any type of object, sculpt the faces of characters, generate settings for your own scenarios, and play trailers or scenes of films, all through the tools offered by the title, tools similar to those made available by the best game engines. *Dreams* in fact has several editors, one for the game scene, one for the story, one for the exhibition, and ones for the characters, sculptures, music, vehicles, and animations. Until now, video games were considered an exclusively vertical medium with a clear line of demarcation between producers and players and the knowledge needed for creating a video game was an insurmountable obstacle for most people, since the IT component is often too steep.

The Media Molecule product breaks down these barriers. In fact anyone who has an excellent idea and a little determination can bring their game to life without having to write a single line. Another peculiarity of *Dreams* is the ability to share each creation with the community, so that anyone can play these games or load them and use them in their own scenes. Organized thematic events, where gamers complete for prizes, are also periodically supported. See Figure 4-3.

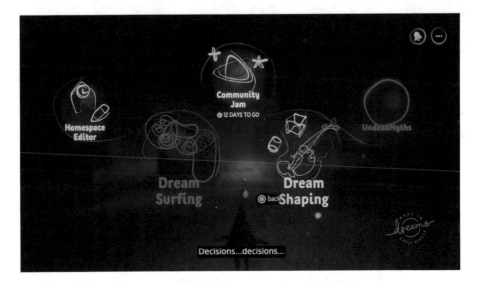

Figure 4-3. *The main menu of the Dreams video game*

Creating a game has always been difficult, and it is important to acknowledge those difficulties and concerns.

Current Problems in the Development of Video Games

Programming, as a computer science, represents the set of activities and techniques that programmers or developers use to implement a program or application, by writing its source code in a certain programming language.

Crunch Time

Crunch time refers to the exhausting working conditions associated with particularly tight delivery times. The big publishers, after setting a release date for a production, actively support the title through huge marketing campaigns and commercial strategies in order to increase *pre-orders,* the purchase of the game before it is actually released, and to optimize profit in the first launch window, which is more profitable.

It often happens, however, that the title is delayed for various reasons. Postponing the release date is a serious risk for the publisher since it must take into account both the turnover in the fiscal year and the reviews of the various communities, increasingly fueled by the culture of *hype.* Hype is generated by the continuous release of trailers, information, and rumors about a certain game.

The simplest solution for a company is to require its employees to extend work hours, often reaching 60, 80, or 100 hours of work per week, to optimize the game as quickly as possible. The crunch forces the developers to live in their offices for long weeks, to work non-stop without interaction with friends and family.

It is a condition that is not bearable long term, carrying the afflicted to depression or voluntary dismissal. The crunch phenomenon was first made public in 2004, when Electronic Arts developer Leander Hasty's partner spoke up publicly about how the tiring pace of work was considered normal at the company and they often did not reap economic rewards. In 2018, Dan Houser, co-founder of Rockstar Games, caused a stir by quietly talking about 100 hours of work per week to complete development by the release date of *Red Dead Redemption 2.* Then, following the reactions of journalists and the public, he retracted the statements by specifying how the extra work from part of the team was volunteer work. *Naughty Dog* chose to postpone the release date of the expected *The Last of* to May 2020, previously scheduled for February.

The publisher declared that the short time available would not have allowed them to guarantee a high level of quality without subjecting the team to stressful hours.

Some industry leaders over the years have decided to leave the big companies to start small, independent teams. Among these are Ken Levine, former creative director of *Irrational Games,* which despite his success with the *Bioshock* series, due to the high stress, he decided to leave the publisher and found the independent *Ghost Story* team.

To combat this problem, several developers have originated *Game Workers United*, an independent organization that brings together various industry professionals. Michele Giannone, co-founder of *Invader Studios* has admitted that the crunch periods were necessary to complete the development of *Daymare*, due to the small number of developers involved.

On the contrary, Antonio Cannata, CEO of *Stormind Games*, criticizes the use of crunch times, blaming the poor organization and poor monitoring of production. In the end, Massimo Guarini of *Ovosonico* considers the crunch the natural result the lack of communication between the development and marketing sectors and justifies its use only if it's properly managed and workers are adequately paid.

Piracy

Video game piracy is a form of copyright infringement that involves the unauthorized copying and distribution of video game software. Developers have tried to counteract video game piracy in many ways. Initially, each copy of a game requires a unique serial key, often found in the manual or in packaging. However, using keygens or no-CD/DVD cracks made this solution useless. Currently, the most effective methods for fighting piracy are Denuvo and the Digital Distribution Services.

- *Denuvo* is an anti-piracy technology for video games. Initially, the protections inserted by this DRM1 in video games were very difficult to overcome, so much so that it forced cracking groups, such as 3DM, to desist. Over time, however, other pirate groups, such as *CPY* or *CODEX*, have managed to violate Denuvo, decreasing its popularity. As stated by Elmar Fisher, sales director of Denuvo Software Solution in an interview at *Games Industry*, the company's philosophy revolves around game protection in the months following release to ensure initial sales and indirectly support the company's revenues. Denuvo is currently facing another problem. According to some benchmarks conducted by *Overlord Gaming,* on the versions with and without Denuvo, the protection system causes heavy performance problems, starting with long loading times to frequent drops in frame rates. Exactly for this reason, some developers, such as *Namco* and *Id Software*, decided to abandon this anti-piracy system.

- The growing popularity of digital distribution services such as Epic Games or Steam has allowed legal copies of video games to attract more players than pirated ones. This is because these services offer very interesting features such as accelerated downloads, cloud saves, automatic patching, and many other features that favor online and co-op modes. In addition, the services regularly deliver the ability to buy video games for free or at a discount. According to Gabe Newell, creator of Steam, it is precisely the addition of these services, rather than that of additional DRM, that discourages piracy.

Despite the fact that piracy remains one of the biggest problems in the gaming industry, it isn't always viewed negatively. An example is represented by Shota Bobokhidze, developer of *Danger Gazers,* who decided to introduce a pirated version of his game on the site. This move generated a 400% increase in sales.

Programming Stages

Before developing any software, be it an application or a video game, you need to know the different stages of programming.

- **Specific.** The program's client describes and defines in a document, as accurately as possible, the problem that must be solved. If the specification is informal, that document contains the desired relationship between input and output data and any constraints to be respected in terms of resources and time. Otherwise, programmers receive a specification that can be represented by a quadruple $S = (X, Y, I, U)$, where X is the set of inputs, i.e. the type of data that the program must expect to be provided, Y is a set of outputs, the type of results that the program must produce, I is the set of conditions to comply to, called preconditions, and U is the set of outgoing conditions, i.e. properties that the program must satisfy. This phase can be difficult, due to abstract work that requires the programmer to imagine the final result and its possible formalizations.

- **Design.** At this stage, the programmer analyzes the problem and conceives in an abstract way a possible algorithm. There are two types of design approaches. Top-down analysis starts with the requirements to solve the problem and breaks them down until reaching elementary problems. Bottom-up analysis combines the elementary problems that can be solved, to find solutions to increasingly complex problems. Finally, a more modern design technique consists of analyzing the problem to identify all relevant elements and their relationships. Those items then are represented in the form of objects.

- **Modeling.** The algorithm is represented in a more formal and detailed way in order to highlight its steps and conceptual structure. In order to complete this phase, several tools can be used, such as flowcharts and pseudocode. Pseudocode is writing the algorithm in a language very similar to the language spoken by the programmer and is structured as a lineup of operations that define the actions to be performed. This stage is very useful for producing documentation.

- **Coding.** During this phase, programmers determine the paradigm of programming that will be used, i.e., the fundamental style of programming. Subsequently, the algorithm is coded in the programming language that best suits the problem to be solved.

- **Verification and correction.** A long process of code testing begins. The program is debugged with the goal of finding and correcting all errors.

Paradigms and Programming Languages

A programming paradigm is "a set of conceptual tools provided by a programming language for writing the source code of a program, thus defining the way in which the programmer conceives and perceives the program itself."

Each programming language leads back to one or more paradigms. Such paradigms differ from each other in the concepts and abstractions used to represent elements of a program, such as variables or functions, and in the procedures used for execution, such as assignments, iterations, or calculation. Generally, a programming paradigm is born by adding new concepts to an existing language and keeping the fundamental concepts intact or putting them in a new perspective. Among the most used paradigms in software development are the following:

- **Modular programming.** Consists of creating programs by dividing them into modules with the aim of simplifying development, testing, and maintenance. These modules perform precise functions, have minimal interaction with the rest of the program, and are independent of each other. *Ada* and *Modula-2* are among the languages specifically oriented for modular programming, but this paradigm is also easily applicable to languages such as C and Assembly.

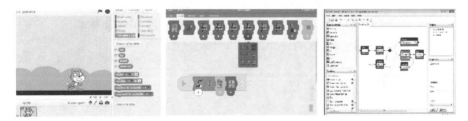

Figure 4-4. *From left to right: sequence, iteration, and selection*

- **Structured programming.** Originates from the criticisms of the structure control which, in the 1960s, represented the fundamental tool for the definition of algorithms, i.e. the unconditional loop, the *goto*. There were two publications that are fundamental for the affirmation of this paradigm: *"Goto statement considered harmful,"* in which Edsger Dijkstra discussed the destructive effects of the Goth on software quality and *"Flow Diagrams, Turing Machines, and Languages with Only Two Formation Rules,"* in which Corrado Bohm and Giuseppe Jacopini showed that any program written using Goth could be rewritten without it, through the use of three types of control structures—sequence, iteration, and selection (see Figure 4-4). Structured languages can admit different control structures, but they must comply with certain fundamental requirements:

  - **Completeness.** They must provide the sequence and at least one structure selection and iteration.

  - **Single point of entry and exit.**

  - **Modularity.** Each structure can have among its instructions other control structures that are recursively controlled.

    Structured programming oriented languages, such as Pascal and C ++, offer a complete set of control structures—that is at least one form of sequence, one of alternative and one of iteration—at the same time keeping the Goth but not recommending its use.

- **Object-oriented programming.** Based on the definition of software objects that interact through the exchange of messages. It adapts to contexts in which it is possible to delineate relationships of interdependence between the concepts to be modeled. This paradigm provides natural support for software modeling of objects of the real world or abstract models to be reproduced. Code is organized into classes in a modular style. A language is object-oriented when it can implement the following mechanisms through its syntax:

  - *Encapsulation.* Involves a separation between the interface of a class and its implementation. In this way, the state interior of an object and the methods that define its logic are accessible to the methods of the object itself, but not to the client (the part of the program that uses it). The purpose of this mechanism is to offer the user functionalities while hiding its implementation.

  - *Inheritance.* Allows you to define classes starting with those already defined. A derived class, while retaining method attributes of the class from which it derives, can define other classes and, through the overriding mechanism, can redefine the inherited method code.

  - *Polymorphism.* Allows you to use the same executable code with instances of different classes having a common superclass. The functionality based on this mechanism is called *dynamic binding* and it allows you to run a particular version of a method based on the type of data contained in the variable at runtime instead of compile time. For example, if a Polygon class contains the area() method, the two subclasses, Square and Rectangle, will redefine the method. The object contained in the variable can therefore be of type Polygon, Rectangle, or Square. When it invokes the area() method on the variable, the version is executed appropriately for the type of object contained in it.

The fundamental elements of this paradigm are classes and objects.

- The *class* is an abstract model that, at the time of code execution, is called to instantiate objects. It's identifiable as a data type abstract that can represent a real object. Inside the class, attributes are defined, variables define the characteristics or properties of objects that can be instantiated by invoking it, and methods are procedures that mirror the behavior of the entity they represent.

- The *object* is an instance of a class and has all the attributes and methods defined in it. Specifically, every object is identified by a certain memory area, in which is stored attributes whose values define the status. Instantiating an object means allocating memory and possibly initializing it. Many languages offer methods called constructors and destructors, which are used to automatically initialize an object and delete it. According to the principle of information hiding, access to the fields of an object must only be allowed through invoked methods on the object itself, thus assigning the complete checking of its state in the class. C ++, Java, and Python are the most common object-oriented programming languages used.

Visual Programming

Visual programming is a way to use visual metaphors to express concepts and it is ideally suited to statistical analysis. It effectively communicates data flow and corresponds to the analysis's emphasis on data. It can naturally reflect non-linear stories and often includes a set of regularly used procedures that fit nicely into the overall structure of statistical analysis.

While it suits statistical analysis far better and overcomes major textual coding concerns, it is not a replacement for everything. Visual programming software products suffer from the same limitation as statistical analysis software, in that they offer users a limited selection of operations.

Scripting languages are frequently used to increase the capabilities of such applications. However, implementing a new function is not the same as stating what should happen to the data at hand. As a result, the benefits of visual programming are lost during the context transfer. As a result, visual programming is not well suited to provide the same level of control that textual coding provides.

A loop or a generic transformation might provide good graphic representations. Because the statement pulls the original column from the data frame, alters it, then writes it back into the same data frame, it may be written as a loop. It may also be seen as a transformation of the complete data frame because the statement converts it from a data frame with a numeric column to one with a quantized column.

The loop representation has the disadvantage of being complicated and difficult to draw. However, seeing it as a data frame transition is an abstraction from the real statement. These issues are the result of an original attempt to visualize the code. According to Myers and Baniassad (2009), this differs from program visualization in that the aim and process are displayed rather than the precise execution. This realization prompted programmers to concentrate more on program transparency.

Unlike other languages that allow programming via written syntax, visual programming languages, also called VPLs, offer the possibility of programming through the graphic manipulation of elements, also allowing, in some cases, the insertion of parts of code. The almost total lack of syntactic rules and the presence of a development environment provides everything programmers need to "design" the program. This makes programming like this easy to learn. Many of these languages are based on the concept of boxes and arrows, where boxes are treated as entities connected by arrows, lines, or arcs, which represent the relationships between them. Furthermore, depending on how they represent functions on-screen, they can be classified as *icon-based, block-based, or diagramming* languages (see Figure 4-5).

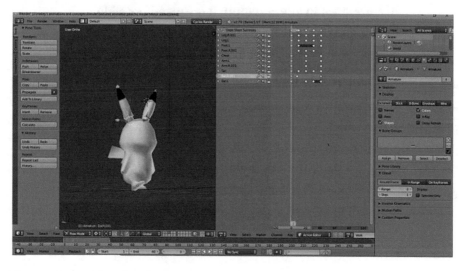

Figure 4-5. *Blender Game Engine- From left to right: block-based*

VPLs, in addition to making programming more accessible, support the programmer on three levels:

- *Syntax.* The use of blocks, shapes, and diagrams tends to reduce and, in some cases, eliminate potential syntactic errors, while they help in the arrangement of primitives and develop well-formed programs.

- *Semantics.* It is possible to find, integrated into the language, several support functions that provide comprehensive documentation of the various primitives.

- *Pragmatic.* VPLs allow you to analyze the behavior of a program in any situation. It is indeed possible to change the status of your entities to observe the reactions of the program to any situation.

An attempt is currently underway to integrate the visual programming approach into data flow-based languages to have immediate access to program status, which involves debugging online and automatic program generation and documentation. As far as the video game sector is concerned, VPLs are at the base, together with scripting languages, of any game engine or game editor (see Figure 4-6).

Figure 4-6. *Blender Game Engine*

The ones discussed next are some of the most commonly used by large development companies and independent companies.

The *Blender Game Engine* is an independent component of *Blender*, written entirely in C ++ by Erwin Coumans and Gino Van Den Bergen, to create a commercial product to develop games and other interactive content, in an artist-friendly way. The engine game uses a graphical interface made up of logical blocks, sensors, controllers, and actuators to control the visualization of objects and their movement. Some games developed through Blender are *Dead Cyborg* and *Yo Frankie!* (see Figure 4-6).

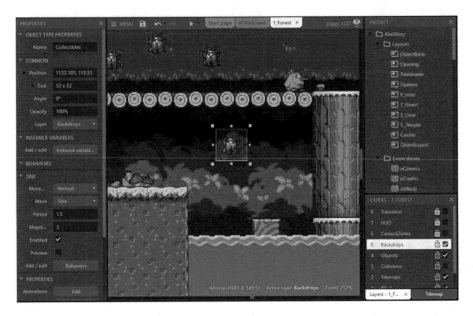

Figure 4-7. *Unity Game Engine*

Unity is a multi-platform game engine developed by *Unity Technologies* (see Figure 4-7). It offers the possibility of developing three-dimensional, two-dimensional, and virtual reality games using a scripting API in C#, which features drag and drop. The engine has also been used outside the gaming industry, for example in the automotive sector, in architecture, and in the cinematic sector. Unity was released in 2005 to make game development accessible to more developers. Among the features currently present are compatibility with web browsers, global illumination in real time, a real-time graphic rendering engine, color grading, analysis of real-time operations and performance reports, timeline for animations, cinemachine, or a camera system intelligent and machine learning tool, such as imitation learning, where the games learn through the real habits of players.

Unity currently supports more than 25 platforms, including PlayStation 4, Nintendo Switch, Mac, iOS, Android, and Steam VR, and it is behind the development of about half of mobile games and about 60% of the contents in augmented and virtual reality.

Among the most popular video games made in Unity are *Temple Run,* a real commercial success, *Ori and The Blind Forest,* a critically acclaimed platform-adventure, *Hollow Knight, Cuphead,* a run-and-gun game inspired by the cartoon style of the 1930s, and *Pokémon GO.*

Figure 4-8. *Construct Game Editor*

Construct is an HTML5-based 2D game editor developed by Scirra Ltd. (see Figure 4-8). Construct is based on event sheets, similar to source files of programming languages. Each event has a list of events, containing conditional statements or triggers, and once satisfied, you can perform actions or functions. The presence of the OR and logical operators, together with the sub-events, allows the development of advanced video games without knowing a language.

Unreal Engine is a graphics engine developed by *Epic Games* and used for the first time in 1998 in *Unreal*. The engine is free to download and Epic allows its use in commercial products, generally asking for 5% of sales revenue. However, with the success of the *Battle Royale Fortnite*, the fee has been eliminated for developers who publish their games through the *Epic Games* Store and suspended for revenues of up to US $1 million.

The engine's native scripting language was UnrealScript, a Java-like language. It was indeed object-oriented, but did not implement multiple inheritance and wrappers for primitive types. With Unreal Engine 4, UnrealScript was removed in favor of C ++, while visual scripts were supported by the Blueprints system.

"One of the key moments in Unreal Engine 4's development was, we had a series of debates about UnrealScript—the scripting language I'd built that we'd carried through three generations. And what we needed to do to make it competitive in the future. And we kept going through bigger and bigger feature lists of what we needed to do to upgrade it, and who could possibly do the work, and it was getting unwieldy. And there was this massive meeting to try and sort it out, and try to cut things and decide what to keep, and plan and ... there was this point where I looked at that and said 'you know, everything you're proposing to add to UnrealScript is already in C ++. Why don lists of what we needed to do to upgrade it, and who could possibly do the work, and it wmum debuggability. It gives us all these advantages."

Tim Sweeney, CEO of Epic Games, 2017

With the release of Unreal Engine 4, Epic Games made a digital marketplace for artists and developers to publish their own creations, such as patterns, sounds, environments, and code snippets, which others might buy, along with tutorials and guides. Epic also provides other content for free, such as assets and tutorials for the game engine. Unreal Engine 5 will be released in late 2021, supporting all existing platforms including next-gen PlayStation 5 consoles and Xbox Series X. Among the main features is *Nanite*, an engine that allows you to import high-level materials into photorealistic details, and *Lumen*, a component that allows fully dynamic global lighting that's immediately responsive to changes in scenes and light. Unreal Engine, in its various versions, has given life to many of the best-known video game sagas. Among them are *BioShock,* a dystopian first-person shooter; the *Batman Arkham* saga, focused on the famous DC superhero; *Borderlands* by Gearbox Software; as well as *Dishonored, Arkane Stealth, Gears of War,* and *Fortnite.*

Godot is another gaming engine that is gaining popularity these days. Godot is a free and open-source 2D and 3D gaming engine distributed under the MIT license. Before its public release, it was created for several firms in Latin America. The development environment is compatible with a variety of operating systems, including Linux, macOS, and Windows.

CryEngine is a gaming engine created by the German software company Crytek, creator of the *Far Cry* and *Crysis* games, among other things. Vehicles, physics, scripting, sophisticated lighting, Polybump technology, shader4, audio 3D, inverse kinematics, real-time soft particle systems, and powerful modular machine intelligence are all supported by the CryEngine. The CryEngine Development Kit SDK, formerly known as Sandbox Editor, is the latest version of Crytek's level editor, and it includes tools for scripting, animations, and object building (see Figure 4-9).

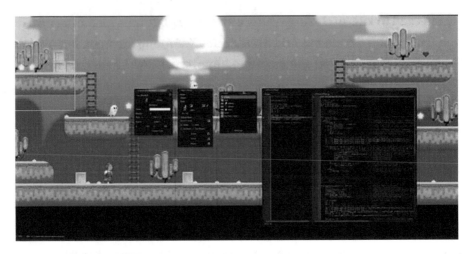

Figure 4-9. *CryEngine*

It uses an additive editing style where the objects are added to a blank space. The presence of the game engine in the editor allows you to easily switch from the editor to the project game in-game. CryEngine has been used to develop numerous titles, among the most famous are *Far Cry*, the *Crysis* series, *Sniper: Ghost Warrior 2, State of Decay, Sonic Boom: Rise of Lyric, Ryse: Son of Rome, Hunt: Showdown,* and *Prey*.

GameMaker is a game engine created by Mark Overmars and developed by *YoYoGames*. It supports cross-platform game development using a drag-and-drop visual programming language or a scripting language compared to JavaScript, called the GameMaker language. It's dedicated to creating games with more advanced features. GameMaker mainly focuses on 2D graphics, allowing immediate use of graphics raster and vector and 2D5 rigging, accompanied by a large library for the creation of 2D graphics and primitives. The 3D graphics options are reserved for more experienced users and are presented in vertex buffer form and matrix functions. Among the games developed with GameMaker are *Risk of Rain*, roguelike in style, *Metroidvania, Nuclear Throne,* a roguelike top-down shooter, *UnderTale,* a J-RPG with multiple endings, and *Hotline Miami*, a critically acclaimed action game.

Summary

The primary issues confronting the gaming industry, publishers, and developers were discussed in this chapter. This chapter also delivered the foundational information needed to understand the following chapter and develop a video game. It covered programming languages and their fundamentals before moving on to visual programming and describing the most commonly used tools in game development: the game engine and game editor. The next chapter covers practical game development using the Python programming language.

CHAPTER 5

Developing a Game in Python

This chapter deals with the development of a real video game. No game engines will be used because that topic is too advanced, but the Python language is used and explained, especially its module, called Pygame.

To illustrate the concepts expressed in the previous chapters, this video game is developed in a visual, integrated development environment using the Python programming language and, in particular, using the Pygame module.

You can access the game's code at:

```
https://github.com/JosephThachilGeorge/TopScan-master
```

Python and Pygame

Python is a dynamic, object-oriented programming language. A dynamic language allows you to perform many operations at runtime, such as type checking, that are commonly done during compilation.

Python was created in the early 90s by Guido Van Rossum and is a multi-paradigm language. It supports object-oriented programming and it possesses many characteristics of functional programming. It is based on three principles: dynamism, simplicity, and flexibility. In addition to

J. T. George and M. J. George, *Human-Computer Interaction in Game Development with Python*, https://doi.org/10.1007/978-1-4842-8182-6_5

Python's similarity to pseudocode, these principles make it one of the first languages studied by those who want to begin programming.

Python has a *standard library*, which is a set of add-on modules that are installed with it to perform specific tasks. Such modules are not immediately active but are loaded through a specified syntax, which is used in the project to load the random, math, and pygame modules. They contain methods to simulate randomness, mathematical functions, and functions related to the development of video games.

```
import random
     import pygame
import math
from pygame.locals import *
```

The pygame module is itself composed of very specialized sub-modules, which are accessible via the following syntax:

pygame.sub-module.

Among these are functions to draw shapes, to load and render fonts (font), to interact with the keyboard (key), to load sounds (mixer), and to work with time.

Designing the Video Game

You must initially collect your ideas and develop a *concept* to define the theme and genre of your video game. The video game in this chapter is influenced by the gameplay of another famous title, *Space Invaders*, a vertical shoot'em up in which a spaceship is positioned at the bottom of the screen. It must save the planet by eliminating dozens of enemies slowly approaching in the sky.

Figure 5-1. *Overview of game design*

The video game, called *TopScan*, uses the same focus and genre, but adds mechanics featured in *Aces of Luftwaffe,* such as the sequential appearance of enemies and the presence of huge bosses at the end of the level. As for the settings, the various levels will have the players flying over a forest, a desert, and finally an ocean.

Development Team

The next step is to identify the roles needed for *TopScan*'s development. Being a 2D video game designed with a purely demonstrative purpose, many important figures presented in Chapter 3, such as the project manager, the 3D modeler, and the animator, are not necessary. The game was also designed by one developer, meaning the different roles involved in game programming, including the roles of concept artist and level designer, were assumed by a single developer.

Game Design Document and Production

The GDD is a document that, as indicated in Chapter 4, must be drawn up before starting the production phase and must contain in particular an analysis of the gameplay, the main elements of the game, and some sketches. The lead designer and/or the level designer is focused on the development of the gameplay, but as previously mentioned, TopScan merges the mechanics of *Space Invaders* and *Aces of Luftwaffe*. It now becomes necessary to write the walkthrough, which is a simple guide on how to complete the game. The one written for *TopScan* is the following:

> "The players find themselves in a spaceship with the purpose of eliminating three powerful bosses and saving the planet. The players can move the spacecraft left and right by pressing the "d" and "a" keys, while with "spacebar" fires bullets. Enemies appear at the top of the screen and, following particular paths, they move downward, where the player is. The players have two ways to survive— they can dodge various enemies or hit them with bullets. Every enemy that's eliminated guarantees a score, which is saved at the end of the level. When players defeat the hordes of enemies, a boss appears, which is a much more offensive opponent and harder to kill."

Finally, in the following paragraphs, the main elements are identified, supporting them with the implementation code and, if present, the graphics.

Game Menu

In *TopScan* there are three menus. There is an initial menu in which players are asked to choose whether to start a new game or continue a previous one they've saved (see Figure 5-2). There is a menu present after defeating the boss, in which the players can save their progress. There is also a menu that pops up when a player is defeated, in which they are informed that the game is over and shown their final score (see Figure 5-3). In the last case, the game remains in wait until a key is pressed by the players, who will then come back to the initial menu.

Figure 5-2. *The TopScan main menu*

The first two screens, in particular, use the drawTextLikeSprite() function, which generates the text as a sprite and exploits a particular method of the Rect objects that establish if the coordinates are inside the object itself.

Figure 5-3. *Game Over screen in TopScan*

Short Introduction to Pygame

Pete Shinners created Pygame, a Python wrapper for SDL. This means you can use Pygame to develop Python games or other multimedia apps that will operate unchanged on any of SDL's supported platforms.

Pygame may be simple to grasp, but the world of graphics programming may be befuddling to the inexperienced. I wrote this to try to condense the practical knowledge I've gathered when working with Pygame and its predecessor, PySDL, over the last year or so. I've attempted to arrange these recommendations in order of priority, but the relevance of any one piece of advice will rely on your background and the specifics of your work.

To utilize Pygame library's methods, you must first import the module:

```
Import pygame
```

These menus are implemented using the following functions:

```
def showGOScreen (score, group, player, background):
    updateGameScreen (background)
    restart (group, player, False)
   drawText (window, "GAME OVER", 64, 660, 300, WHITE, False)
   drawText (window, "Press key back to start menu", 18, 670,
   500, False)
   drawText (window, "Score: {}". format (score), 48, 735,
   400, WHITE, False)
   waiting = True
while waiting:
    updateScreen ()
   for ev in pygame.event.get ():
            if ev.type == pygame.QUIT or ev.type == KEYDOWN and
            ev.key == K_ESCAPE:
                    pygame.quit ()
                    if ev.type == pygame.KEYDOWN:
    waiting = False

def mainMenu ():
    global level, score
    game = True
    while game:
        for ev in pygame.event.get ():
        if ev.type == pygame.QUIT or ev.type == KEYDOWN
        and ev.key == K_ESCAPE:
            pygame.quit ()
            elif ev.type == MOUSEBUTTONDOWN and ev.button == 1:
            click = if necessary
            if newGame.rect.collidepoint (click):
                score = 0
                level = 1
```

```
            levels (level)
        elif toContinue.rect.collidepoint (click):
            str = ""
            savedata = open ("savedata.txt", "r")
            capture = savedata.readline ()
            for char in range (len (capture)):
            if capture [char] .isdecimal () == True:
            str = str + capture [char]
            level = int (str)
            str = ""
            capture = savedata.readline ()
            for char in range (len (capture)):
            if capture [char] .isdecimal () == True:
            str = str + capture [char]
            score = int (str)
            savedata.close ()
            levels (level)
    newGame = drawTextLkSprite (screen, text, "New Game",
    32, 1000, 570)
    toContinue = drawTextLkSprite (screen, text, "Cont",
    32, 1000, 620)
    text.draw (window)
```

Game Interface

As a UI programmer, it was necessary to define a specification for
TopScan's user interface, i.e. a system that allows communication between
the players and the game. It was therefore decided to create a non-
diegetic one that's external to the game world with data superimposed on
the screen.

- The drawShield() function is used to show the shield of the player and the life of the boss. It comes initially drawn in an outer rectangle and then is filled with an inner one, based on the percentage of life or shield present. The flag is used to choose whether to show the name of the boss or the shield symbol.

```
def drawShield (surface, x, y, percentage, image, flag,
maxLife):
    if flag:
    drawText (surface, name, 36, x - 20, y - 12, WHITE, True)
else:
    image = pygame.transform.scale (image, (20, 20))
    surface.blit (image, (x - 30, y))
if percentage <0:
percentage = 0
length = 200
height = 20
fill = (percentage / maxLife) * length
outlineRect = pygame.Rect (x, y, length, height)
fillRect = pygame.Rect (x, y, fill, height)
pygame.draw.rect (surface, RED, fillRect)
pygame.draw.rect (surface, WHITE, outlineRect, 4)
```

- The score increases based on the value of a particular attribute of each defeated enemy and has the pure purpose of creating healthy competition between different players. The drawText() function takes advantage of the font module to draw the score on the screen.

```python
def drawText (surface, text, size, x, y, color, flag):
    font = pygame.font.SysFont ("Arial", size, bold = True)
    textSurface = font.render (text, True, color)
    textRect = textSurface.get_rect ()
    surface.blit (textSurface, textRect)
```

The players' lives, closely linked to one of their attributes, are represented by the thumbnails positioned on the right side of the game. The drawLives() function generates a surface with the chosen image and, using the blit() method, associates it with a rect, an abstract area with the same dimensions as the surface, used to place the object.

```python
def drawLives (surface, x, y, lives, image):
    for i in range (lives):
        image = pygame.transform.smoothscale (image, (30, 30))
        imageRect = image.get_rect ()
        imageRect.right = x
        imageRect.bottom = y - 50 * i
        surface.blit (image, imageRect)
```

The Player

As mentioned, the player in *TopScan* controls a spaceship implemented by the Player class, a subclass of pygame.sprite.Sprite. The speed of the spacecraft has been implemented by changing each screen's position on the x axis. In addition to speed, other parameters are defined, such as the value of the shield, the number of lives, the number of bullets fired (numBull), and the maximum number of bullets present at the same time on the screen (maxNumBull).

The update() method updates the player's position and the
duration of powerup speed and newGun, using the faster, speed-Timer,
numTwoShot, and numThreeShot variables. Finally, the hidden and
hideTimer variables manage the disappearance/appearance effect present
when the shield of the players drop to 0 and they consequently lose a life.

```python
class Player (pygame.sprite.Sprite):
    def __init__ (self, image):
        pygame.sprite.Sprite .__ init __ (self)
        self.image = image
        self.rect = image.get_rect ()
        self.velx = 5
    self.shield = 100
    self.lives = 3
    self.maxLife = 100
    self.numBull = 1
    self.maxNumBull = 5
    self.numTwoShot = 0
    self.numThreeShot = 0
    self.shootDelay = 400
    self.lastShot = pygame.time.get_ticks ()
    self.hidden = False
    self.hideTimer = pygame.time.get_ticks ()
    self.faster = False
    self.speedTimer = pygame.time.get_ticks ()

def update (self):
    if self.numBull == 3 and self.numThreeShot> 5:
        self.numBull = 1
        self.numThreeShot = 0
    elif self.numBull == 2 and self.numTwoShot> 5:
        self.numBull = 1
        self.numTwoShot = 0
```

```
if self.hidden and pygame.time.get_ticks () - self.hide Timer>
500: self.hidden = False self.rect.topleft = (320, 500) self.
shield = 100
if self.faster and pygame.time.set_ticks () - self.speedTimer>
POWUP: self.faster =
False self.velx = 5

keystate = pygame.key.get_pressed ()
if keystate [pygame.K_a] or keystate [pygame.K_LEFT]:
    if self.velx> 0:
        self.velx * = -1
self.rect.x + = self.velx
elif keystate [pygame.K_d] or keystate [pygame.K_RIGHT]:
    if self.velx <0:
        self.velx * = -1
    self.rect.x + = self.velx

if self.rect.right> screen.get_width ():
    self.rect.right = screen.get_width ()
elif self.rect.left <0:
    self.rect.left = 0

def shoot (self, image):
    now = pygame.time.get_ticks ()
    if now - self.lastShot> self.shootDelay:
        self.lastShot = now
        if self.numBull == 1:
            self.shootDelay = 400
            bullet = Bullet (self.rect.centerx, self.rect.
            top, image)
            allSprites.add (bullet)
            bullets.add (bullet)
```

```
if self.numBull == 2:
        self.shootDelay = 200
        bullet1 = Bullet (self.rect.left, self.rect.
        centery, image)
        bullet2 = Bullet (self.rect.right, self.rect.
        centery, image)
    allSprites.add (bullet1)
    allSprites.add (bullet2)
    bullets.add (bullet1)
    bullets.add (bullet2)
    self.numTwoShot + = 1
```

Powering Up

The images corresponding to the powerups present in the game are loaded and inserted into the poweImage list.

```
poweImage = {}
poweImage ["speed"] = pygame.image.load ("Image / Player /
speed.png")
poweImage ["shield"] = pygame.image.load ("Image / Player /
shield.png")
poweImage ["extra"] = pygame.image.load ("Image / Player /
extraLife.png")
poweImage ["toxic"] = pygame.image.load ("Image / Player /
toxic.png")
poweImage ["newGun"] = pygame.image.load ("Image / Player /
newGun.png")
```

The power class, a subclass of pygame.sprite.Sprite, generates the powerup instances by randomly choosing the type, using the random method called choice() at creation time. The update() method instead updates the movement of the powerups on the y axis.

```
class Power (pygame.sprite.Sprite):
def __init__ (self, center):
    pygame.sprite.Sprite .__ init __ (self)
    self.type = random.choice (["shield", "speed", "extra",
    "toxic", "newGun"])
    self.image = pygame.transform.smoothscale (poweImage
    [self.type], (40, 40))
    self.rect = self.image.get_rect ()
    self.rect.center = center
    self.vely = 5
def update (self):
self.rect.y + = self.vely
if self.rect.top> screen.get_height ():
self.kill ()
```

The usePowerUp() function implements the effect that certain enhancements have in the game. The shield grants 20 additional shield points, speed increases the player's speed for a short time, extra and toxic respectively add and take a life away from the player, and newGun increases the number of bullets fired at the same time.

```
def usePowerUp (power, player):
    if power.type == "shield":
        if player.shield <100:
            player.shield + = 20
                if player.shield> 100:
                    player.shield = 100

    elif power.type == "speed":
        player.velx = 10
        player.faster = True
        player.speedTimer = pygame.time.get_ticks ()
```

```
elif power.type == "extra":
    if player.lives <5:
        player.lives + = 1

elif power.type == "toxic":
    if player.lives> 1:
        player.lives - = 1

    elif power.type == "newGun":
        player.numBer + = 1
```

Finally, the powerups are drawn to the screen when an enemy is eliminated. However, to simulate the randomness of the action, they are created only when the random.random() method returns a number greater than 0.7.

```
if random.random ()> 0.7:
power = Power (hit.rect.center)
all Sprites.add (power)
power.and (power)
```

The Enemies

The Enemy class represents the prototype of the enemy present in *TopScan*. It is then extended by several subclasses, including Invaders, Rollers, and Rare. Among their attributes are their number of lives, the damage inflicted, and the score obtained by the player upon elimination of the enemy (score). The update() method updates the enemy's position on the screen. This is usually rewritten in subclasses to allow for different enemies to follow alternate trajectories of movement.

```
class Enemy (pygame.sprite.Sprite):
def __init __ (self, image, position, name, lives,
damage, score):
    pygame.sprite.Sprite .__ init __ (self)
    self.image = image
    self.rect = image.get_rect ()
    self.rect.bottomleft = position
    self.name = "none"
    self.velx = 0
    self.vely = 0
    self.lives = lives
    self.damage = damage
    self.score = score
def update (self):
    self.rect.x + = self.velx
    self.rect.y + = self.vely
    if self.rect.top> screen.get_height ():
    self.kill ()
```

As an example of such subclasses, let's analyze Rollers. This class
inherits the attribute's lives, damage, and score from the Enemy class.
However, it also updates the update() method, which by doing so allows
these objects to follow a zigzag trajectory. This trajectory is made possible
by updating the positions of the enemies on the x and y axes at the same
time and using a new variable, called offset, to control its rebound point.

```
class Rollers (Enemy):
def __init __ (self, image, position, vel, lives, damage,
score, offset):
    super () .__ init __ (image, position, name, lives,
    damage, score)
    self.velx = vel [0]
    self.vely = vel [1]
```

```
        self.name = "Roller"
        self.offset = offset

def update (self):
    if self.velx> 0:
            self.rect.x + = self.velx
            self.rect.y = self.rect.x / 4 + self.offset
            if self.rect.right> screen.get_width ():
                self.velx * = -1
                self.offset + = 355
        elif self.velx <0:
            self.rect.x + = self.velx
            self.rect.y = -self.rect.x / 4 + self.offset
            if self.rect.left <0:
                self.velx * = -1
if self.rect.top> screen.get_height ():
    self.kill ()
```

The Bosses

As with enemies, bosses in *TopScan* are spawned by subclasses of the
Boss class, which defines their lives (lives), the damage inflicted on the
players (damage), the score obtained by eliminating the boss (score), and
four other attributes used in the shoot() and obstaclesAtk() methods:
lastShot, lastObstacles, existsObstacles, and obstaclesDelay.

```
class Boss (pygame.sprite.Sprite):
    def __init __ (self, image, position, lives, maxLife,
    damage, score, vel):
        pygame.sprite.Sprite .__ init __ (self)
        self.image = image
        self.rect = image.get_rect ()
```

155

```
            self.rect.midleft = position
            self.lives = lives
            self.maxLife = maxLife
            self.damage = damage
            self.score = score
            self.velx = vel [0]
            self.vely = vel [1]
            self.split = False
            self.lastShot = pygame.time.get_ticks ()
            self.lastObstacles = pygame.time.get_ticks ()
            self.existsObstacles = False
            self.obstaclesDelay = 50000
def update (self):
     self.rect.x + = self.velx
     self.rect.y + = self.vely
def hit (self):
     pass
def shoot (self):
     pass
def obstaclesAtk (self):
     pass
```

It is now necessary to analyze the three subclasses that implement the three bosses endings. These classes have a very similar structure, but the bosses possess unique characteristics, such as the type of movement and attack style. For this reason, only methods implement these features.

Movement. The first boss, Gorgodusa, uses the movement method contained in the Enemy class, so it can move from the right to the left, changing direction as it makes contact with the left or right side of the screen.

Conversely, the *Golem* boss moves along a zigzag trajectory, implemented by the following code. The screen is ideally divided into intervals corresponding to the different trajectories necessary to simulate movement. The displacements in these intervals are stored in counter, which resets when one of the limits has been reached. fall instead provides a limit to the length of the trajectory diagonally, while molt is used to manage its inclination.

```python
def update(self):
    if self.rect.left < 0:
        self.rect.left = 0
        self.velx *= -1
        self.right = True
    elif self.rect.right > screen.get_width():
        self.rect.right = screen.get_width()
        self.velx *= -1
        self.right = False

        self.rect.x += self.velx
        self.rect.y = self.set - self.molt * self.counter * \
        self.inversion
        self.counter += self.velx

if self.rect.y <= self.position[1] - 100:
    self.set = self.position[1] - 99
    if self.right:
        self.inversion = -1
    else:
        self.inversion = 1
    self.counter = 0
elif self.rect.y >= self.position[1] + self.fall:
    self.set = self.position[1] + self.fall - 1
```

```
    if self.right:
        self.inversion = 1
    else:
        self.inversion = -1
        self.counter = 0
```

The last boss, Bidramon, uses a lot of movement similar to that of the sine function of x, and it is precisely through the sin() method of the math module that we can simulate its pace. position is instead used to store the position on the y axis, where the boss comes into contact with the right or left side of the screen.

```
def update (self):
    if self.rect.left <0 and self.velx <0:
        self.rect.left = 0
        self.velx * = -1
    elif self.rect.right> screen.get_width () and self.
    velx> 0:
        self.rect.right = screen.get_width ()
        self.velx * = -1
    self.rect.x + = self.velx
        if self.velx> 0:
            self.rect.y = self.position [1] +
            math.sin (self.rect.x * math.pi * screen.get_
            width () / 100 /
             (screen.get_width () - self.image.get_width
             ())) * 50
        elif self.velx <0:
            self.rect.y = self.position [1] -
            math.sin (self.rect.x * math.pi * screen.get_
            width () / 100 /
             (screen.get_width () - self.image.get_width
             ())) * 50
```

The Hit() method defines the different boss reactions based on the amount of damage suffered. Each boss has three or four stages: soft, medium, hard, or critical damage, each of which modifies various attributes, such as stamina, the waiting time between attacks, the number of projectiles generated, etc. The three bosses have special attacks once their life has reached a critical level. Gorgodusa decreases the player's speed attribute, simulating a slowdown in time for the player. Golem decreases the value of its fall attribute, so as to swoop into the player. Finally, Bidramon, once its life drops to 200 life points, will disappear. Then it generates two minibosses, both implemented by the Bidramon class and therefore able to move and attack like Bidramon.

```
def hit(self):
    \# soft damage
    if self.lives == 310:
        self.shotDelay = 1500

        \# hard damage
        elif self.lives == 220:
            self.obstaclesAtk()
            self.obstaclesDelay = 4000

        \# critical damage
        elif self.lives == 100:
            self.shotDelay = 800
            player.velx = 2

def hit(self):
    \# soft damage
    if self.lives == 400:
        self.numBull = 12

    \# hard damage
    elif self.lives == 200:
```

```
            self.resistence = 30
            self.obstaclesAtk()
            self.obstaclesDelay = 5000

    \# critical damage
    elif self.lives == 100:
            self.numBull = random.randrange(10, 16, 2)
            self.fall = 400
            self.molt = 4
def hit(self):
    \# soft damage
        if self.lives == 500:
            self.shotDelay = 1400
        \# medium damage
        elif self.lives == 400:
            self.shotDelay = 1200

        \# hard damage
        elif self.lives == 300:
            self.obstaclesAtk()
            self.obstaclesDelay = 6000
        \# critical damage
        elif self.lives == 200:
            self.kill()
            self.split = True
```

The shoot() method simply defines the main mode in which the boss attacks. The different bullets are all managed by the class EnemyBullet, which determines the bullet's speed and the damage dealt to the player. The update() method updates the position of the bullets based on the direction's attribute value. In particular, the bullets of the sin type used by Bidramon move by randomly modifying the axis of origin and the amplitude of the wave.

```
class EnemyBullet (pygame.sprite.Sprite):
    def __init __ (self, x, y, image, vel, direction, damage):
        pygame.sprite.Sprite .__ init __ (self)
        self.image = image
        self.rect = image.get_rect ()
        self.rect.bottom = y
        self.rect.centerx = x
        self.direction = direction
        self.velx = vel [0]
    self.vely = vel [1]
    self.damage = damage
    self.sinAxis = x
self.gap = random.randrange (50, 150, 10)

def update(self):
    if self.direction == "center":
        self.rect.y += self.vely
    elif self.direction == "right":
        self.rect.x += self.velx
        self.rect.y += self.vely
    elif self.direction == "left":
        self.rect.x += self.velx
        self.rect.y += self.vely
    elif self.direction == "sin":
        self.rect.y += self.vely
        self.rect.x = self.sinAxis + math.sin(self.
        rect.y*math.pi*
            screen.get_height()/100/(screen.get_height() -
                self.image.get_height()))*self.gap
```

```
            if self.rect.x < self.sinAxis + 5 and self.rect.
            x>self.sinAxis-5:
                  self.gap = random.randrange(50, 150, 10)
    if self.rect.bottom < 0:
         self.kill()
```

Figure 5-6 shows the attack of Gorgodusa.

The obstacles k() method, like the previous one, defines an alternate boss attack. Through the Obstacles class, there is a subclass of pygame. sprite.Sprite. The owner identifies the boss who generated the obstacle and represents the damage inflicted on the player by the obstacle. False prevents the obstacle from damaging the player, while damageDelay and timeToNew Damage prevent the player from taking continuous damage from obstacles.

```
class Obstacles (pygame.sprite.Sprite):
def __init__ (self, position, image, vely, damage,
damageDelay, owner):
    pygame.sprite.Sprite .__ init __ (self)
    self.image = image
    self.rect = image.get_rect ()
    self.rect.centerx = position [0]
    self.rect.top = position [1]
    self.vely = vely
    self.owner = owner
    .dangerous = True
    self.damage = damage
    self.damageDelay = damageDelay
    self.timeToNewDamage = pygame.time.get_ticks ()
    self.back = False
```

```python
def update (self):
    if self.owner == "Gorgodusa":
        if self.rect.y <= 300:
            self.back = True
            self.vely = 1
        elif self.rect.top> screen.get_height () + 20:
            self.kill ()

        if not self.back:
            self.rect.y - = self.vely
        else:
            self.rect.y + = self.vely
    elif self.owner == "Golem" or self.owner == "Bidramon":
        self.rect.y + = self.vely
        if self.rect.top> screen.get_height ():
            self.kill ()

def hitPlayer (self):
    self.dangerous = False
    now = pygame.time.get_ticks ()

    if now - self.timeToNewDamage> self.damageDelay:
        self.dangerous = True
```

Collision Management

Serving as the role of physics programmer, it was necessary to establish
the interaction among the various elements that make up the game. These
parts of code are very similar to each other and are based on insertion
in a list of the object that caused a collision, be it a bullet, an enemy, or
an obstacle. Then they perform various actions such as damaging the
player, eliminating the enemy, making the bullets disappear, or exploiting
the attributes of the elements in the list. In particular, the player can take

damage due to direct contact with an enemy, with an opponent's bullet, or with an obstacle generated from a boss. Enemies and the boss take damage if hit by the player or by bullets, and are eliminated if their life drops to 0.

To detect collisions, Pygame has built-in methods such as groupcollide and spritecollide. Basic collision detection in PyGame may be accomplished with Pygame. The Rect object has several ways for detecting object collisions with objects that are rectangular.

It is worth noting that the collision of a rectangular item with a circular object, such as a paddles and a ball in the *Pong* game, may be roughly detected by a collision of two rectangular objects, the paddle and the ball's enclosing rectangle.

The bullets disappear upon contact with enemies and other projectiles, dealing damage in the first case. The contact between obstacles and bullets causes the disappearance of the bullets.

```
hits = pygame.sprite.groupcollide (allEnemies, bullets,
False, True)
    for hit in hits:
        hit.lives - = 1
        if hit.lives <= 0:
            updateDex (enemyDex, hit.name)
            score + = hit.score
            hit.kill ()

hits = pygame.sprite.spritecollide (player, obstacles, False)
    for hit in hits:
        if hit.dangerous:
            hit.hitPlayer ()
            player.shield - = hit.damage
            hit.timeToNewDamage = pygame.time.get_ticks ()
            if player.shield <= 0:
                player.shield = 0
                player.lives - = 1
```

```
            if player.lives == 0:
                done = True
                win = False
            player.hide ()
for boss in bosses:
    hits = pygame.sprite.spritecollide (boss, bullets, True)
        for hit in hits:
            boss.live - = (hot.boy Damage - boss.resistant)
            boss.hit ()
            if boss.lives <= 0:
                score + = boss.score
                    update Dex (enemy Dex, boss.name)
                    boss.kill ()done = True
                    win = True
```

The Levels

Finally, as a level designer, it was necessary to focus on constructing the game levels. Given the genre and simplicity of the game, the individual levels were generated by loading a background image and inserting it in the surface containing the playing area, by using the update Game Screen() function.

```
def updateGameScreen (background):
    window.blit (title, ((20, 20)))
    window.blit (border, ((window.get_width () - 820) /1.2,
        (window.get_height () - 620) /1.5))
    border.fill (YELLOW)
    border.blit (screen, (10, 10))
    title.blit (titleImg, (0, 0))
    screen.blit (background, (0, 0))
```

The next step was to choose the Spawn's points and times of the different enemies. Analyzing the next code, represented in the first level, it can be seen that this was made possible by using a `for` loop that's capable of analyzing different events. Five timers were also set, through the pygame time module, each of which is responsible for a customized event.

In the following situation, the first event spawns up to ten `invader` enemies, then resets the first counter and the first timer and activates the second. This object generates the `USEREVENT + 2` event, which is responsible for the creation of 14 `rollers`. In doing so, it finally generates the boss when `USEREVENT + 4` shows up.

```python
for ev in pygame.event.get ():
    if ev.type == USEREVENT + 1:
        if level == 1:
            if numEnemy1 <10:
                pygame.time.set_timer (USEREVENT + 1,
                    random.randrange (700, 1000))
                invader = Invader (enemy1Img, (random.
                randrange (0,
                    screen.get_width () - 98 + 1), -1), (0, 4),
                    1, 10, 10)
                allEnemies.add (invader)
                numEnemy1 + = 1
            elif numEnemy1 == 10:
                pygame.time.set_timer (USEREVENT + 1, 0)
                pygame.time.set_timer (USEREVENT + 2, 1500)
                numEnemy1 = 0

    elif ev.type == USEREVENT + 2:
        if level == 1:
            if numEnemy2 <14:
                pygame.time.set_timer (USEREVENT + 2,
                    random.randrange (2000, 3000))
```

```
                        rollers1 = Rollers (enemy2Img, (0, -1),
                        (4, 0), 2, 20, 20, 0)
                        allEnemies.add (rollers1)
                        numEnemy2 + = 1
                        rollers2 = Rollers (enemy2Img, (screen.
                        get_width () -
                            98 + 1, -1), (4, 0), 2, 20, 20, -180)
                        allEnemies.add (rollers2)
                        numEnemy2 + = 1

                elif numEnemy2 == 14:
                        pygame.time.set_timer (USEREVENT + 2, 0)
                        pygame.time.set_timer (USEREVENT + 3, 8000)
                        numEnemy2 = 0
        elif ev.type == USEREVENT + 3:
            if level == 1:
                if numEnemy1 <10:
                        pygame.time.set_timer (USEREVENT + 3,
                            random.randrange (900, 1200))
                        invader = Invader (enemy1Img, (random.randrange
                            (0, screen.get_width () - 98 + 1), -1),
                            (0, 4), 2, 30, 20)
                        allEnemies.add (invader)
                        numEnemy1 + = 1
        elif numEnemy1 == 10:
            pygame.time.set_timer (USEREVENT + 3, 0)
                pygame.time.set_timer(USEREVENT + 4, 7000)
        elif ev.type == USEREVENT + 4:
            if level == 1:
                if not existsBoss:
                        boss = Gorgodusa(bossImg, (400, 75), 400, 400,
                        30, 150, (5, 0), "Gorgodusa")
```

```
                bosses.add(boss)
                existsBoss = True
        elif level == 2:
            if not existsBoss:
                boss = Golem(bossImg2, (400, 75), 500, 500,
                30, 250, (3, 0), "Golem")
                bosses.add(boss)
                existsBoss = True
        elif level == 3:
            if not existsBoss:
                boss = Bidramon(bossImg3, (400, 75), 600,
                600, 30, 400, (5, 0), "Bidramon")
                bosses.add(boss)
                existsBoss = True

    elif ev.type == USEREVENT + 5:
        if level == 1:
            rare = Rare(pygame.image.load("Image/Enemies/
            enemyShip.png"),
                    (-1, random.randrange(ciao.get_height(),
                        screen.get_width()/2, 10)), 1, 150)
            allEnemies.add(rare)
        pygame.time.set_timer(USEREVENT+5,random.
        randrange(25000,35000))
```

Figures 5-4 through 5-6 show screens from TopScan's various levels of gameplay.

Figure 5-4. *TopScan's ship engaged against the Mothsions in Level 1*

Figure 5-5. *TopScan's ship engaged against the Shinopines in Level 1*

Figure 5-6. *The Gorgodusa boss attacks!*

Summary

By creating this project, you have observed the different aspects of game development. Developing video games turns out to be one of the most difficult aspects in the field of computers. Having basic knowledge is often not enough to be successful. Competition is fierce and standards are high, and few games manage to emerge or get noticed by large publishers.

Currently however, smaller teams and individuals can take advantage of offers by free game engines, which simplify some aspects of the design. They can also take advantage of crowdfunding platforms, which offer the possibility of obtaining funding and initiatives run by publishers, such as Sony, Microsoft, and Steam with Greenlight, which provides a showcase to get visibility and financial support for promising projects.

TopScan development offers a first approach to the world of game development. However, the lack of a team to share the work with and singular use of Python slowed development and prevented the creation of a more complete and complex work.

While developing games, it is necessary to use human-computer interaction techniques in order to increase their effectiveness. Many people have attempted to define gamification throughout the years. Other accounts are more well-known than others, and in some situations, a particular aspect of the phenomena is given more weight. We describe flowchart diagrams for basic game interface design in the following chapter.

CHAPTER 6

Game Development – Industry Standards

You learned how to develop a game using the HCI approach in the previous chapter. In the gaming industry, however, each supplier develops a game using proprietary technologies. How can you construct a broad design and architecture for game development in this case? That is what you will learn in this chapter. You learn how to employ generic patterns in game design.

This chapter focuses on the following points

- Overall design of a game from frontend and backend
- Sequence diagram for the game development cycle
- Security of online games through a web portal

Game Terminology

Before you get started, you need to familiarize yourself with some of the terminology used in this chapter:

- **Player:** A person who engages in video games or computer games.

© Joseph Thachil George, Meghna Joseph George 2022
J. T. George and M. J. George, *Human-Computer Interaction in Game Development with Python*, https://doi.org/10.1007/978-1-4842-8182-6_6

- **Web portal:** A specifically built website that collects data from a variety of sources, such as emails, online forums, and search engines, and presents it in a unified fashion. In this scenario, players log in using their credentials in order to play a certain game.

- **Cashier:** Four tasks are performed by the cashier in the game.

1) Audits money drawers and counts money.

2) Keeps detailed records of all monetary transactions, authorization papers, and reconciliations.

3) Creates change for clients and exchanges cash, credit cards, and game/casino chips.

4) Works in and monitors a designated area on the game/casino floor with the gambling machines.

Overall Design of the Game

This section looks at the game's frontend and backend from the perspective of the player.

Frontend and Backend in Game Development

Application design has become a diversified field as emerging innovations develop, and new boundaries are discovered. The distinction between frontend, backend, and game design has grown perplexing. Modern-day devices, Internet of Things ideas, mobile apps, video game for consoles, browser-based applications (plug-ins/extensions), web applications, frontend development, desktop applications, UI/UX designers, and game designers of all different fields have all become part of the development process. These domains are now completely self-contained, and one might pursue one route of growth without contemplating any other. Let's look at the significant distinctions between all of them.

The frontend development and game development are two very distinct things. To enter into game development, you'll need particular design talents as well as a distinct set of tools and technology.

Frontend programming, on the other hand, is concerned with the appearance of web applications and websites. JQuery, AngularJs, ReactJs, VueJs, KnockoutJs, BackboneJs, and many more libraries and frameworks are often used to program content to show on a website using JavaScript and many of its frameworks and tools. As technologies get better, new initiatives are being introduced, and software behemoths are attempting to dominate the market by providing something significant that has the potential to change the game. Visual Basic VB Studio was originally intended for desktop applications. Microsoft renamed it Visual Studio to cover the same design concepts and developed a new program line to compete with Sun's Java, which was the technology giant at the time.

Different frontend frameworks are now being used. The open-source community is incredibly active, and they are constantly developing new libraries, frameworks, and platforms. NodeJs was created to aid developers in using the same frontend JavaScript expertise to create backend web applications.

Verify the Token

For authentication and authorization, games services employs the OAuth 2.0 protocol, which supports a wide range of scenarios for web servers and client-side apps. Customized grant types have also been created by Epic for a few unique situations.

When you begin, you'll need to get Epic's OAuth 2.0 client keys. When obtaining an authentication token from the Epic authorization server, they will be in the form of a Client ID and Client Secret. For additional information, see the Getting Started with Epic Account Management page.

A one-use swap code will be used to authenticate the game client with Epic's authentication server when it is initiated from the Epic Games Store. The Epic Launcher generates this exchange code, which is then supplied to the gaming client as a control option.

The gaming client will send a request to the Epic token's API with the client keys and exchange the code when it is started.

All queries to Epic services will contain the access token from the gaming client. The identifier can also be used in service-to-service calls or supplied to trusted gaming servers for authentication.

A refresh token will be supplied in the token response if it is relevant. If the access token expires, the game client must utilize a refresh token. This usually happens within two hours of receiving the authentication token.

So basically, we use two type of token—one is a general token and the other is an access token (SSO token).

The ID token is a security token that holds information about an end user and is issued by the OpenID provider. Access tokens, on the other hand, aren't meant to convey personal information. They merely grant access to particular server resources that have been specified.

In general, any game service provider employs a set of common services in the production of their games. These services can be developed with any backend programming languages (see Table 6-1). Basically, if the game involves money, the services listed in the table are unquestionably required in the game's design. These services can be implemented in any computer language, such as Java or Python.

Table 6-1. *General Description of the Services*

Service Name	Calling System	Interaction Description
Table Registration	Game Engine	Called by the game engine before starting to accept players to the table
Game Session Start	Game Engine	Called by the game engine before accepting the single player to the table
Add Funds	Game Engine	Called by the game engine before moving more money from the customer's e-wallet to the table
Add Funds Cancellation	Game Engine	Called by the game engine every time a request to add funds must be cancelled
Game Session End	Game Engine	Called by the game engine to close the player game session
Table End	Game Engine	Called by the game engine to close the table
User Authentication	Game Engine	Called by the game engine to authenticate the user
Verify Token	Game Engine	Called by the game engine to verify the validity of the token
User Balance	Game Engine	Called by the game engine to retrieve the e-wallet balance of the user
User LogOff	Game Engine	Called by the game engine to invalidate the token

1. verifyToken(): Called by the game engine to verify the validity of the token. If the game engine provides game clients that do not ask for user credentials, then the game engine can use the "Verify Token" method described hereafter (see Figure 6-1).

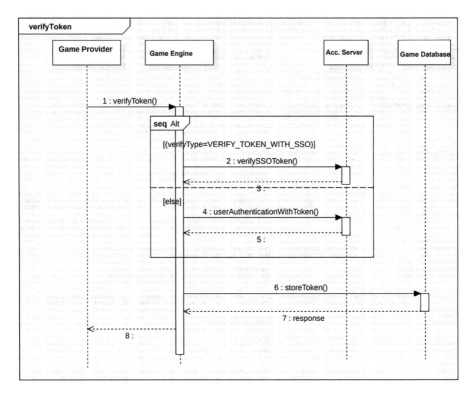

Figure 6-1. *Verify token*

This API is called from the game engine to test the validity of the token returned by the authentication's API.

2. `userAuthentication()`: Called by the game engine to authenticate the user. If the game engine provides game clients that are asking for user credentials, then the game engine can use the "User Authentication" method described hereafter. The game client has to call this service and provide all the user credentials (username and password). It then receives the nickname to be used in

the tables and the chat in case of successful authentication. The game client will also pass input to the operator owner of the user account. The nickname returned will be unique to the whole network (see Figure 6-2).

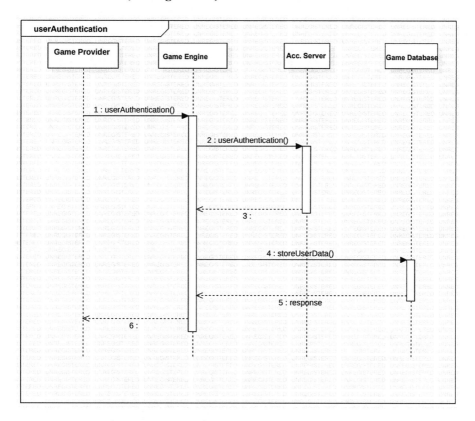

Figure 6-2. *User authentication*

3. userBalance(): Called by the game engine to retrieve the e-wallet balance of the user. After the "User Authentication" call, the game client has to ask the game engine for the amount of money in the user's game (see Figure 6-3).

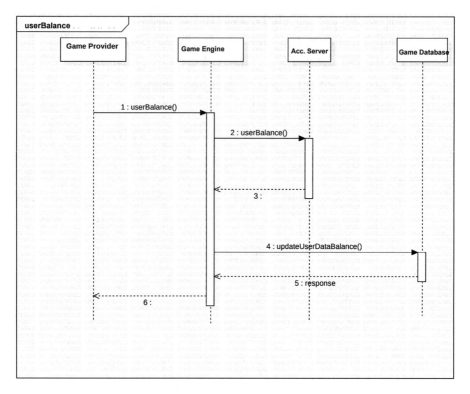

Figure 6-3. *User balance*

4. `tableRegistration()`: Called by the game engine
   before accepting players to the table. Tables of a
   given type are always available for seating; when
   the first player sits down, the game engine spawns
   a new empty instance of the same table type (see
   Figure 6-4).

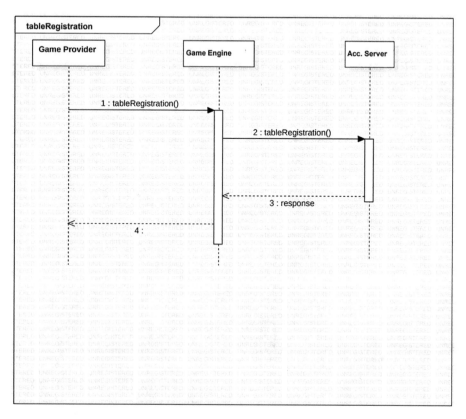

Figure 6-4. *Table registration*

5. gameSessionstart(): Called by the game engine
   before accepting a player to the table. Before
   accepting a user to the game table, the game engine
   has to call this service and provide all the game's
   session parameters (see Figure 6-5).

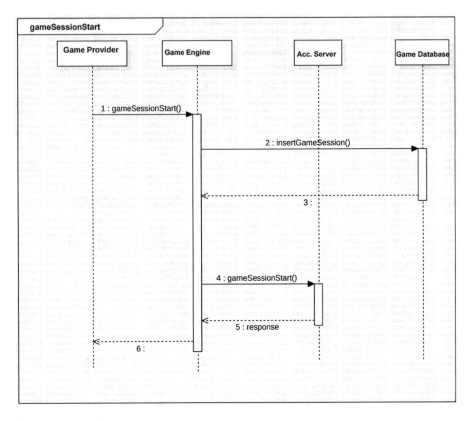

Figure 6-5. *Game session start*

6. gameSessionEnd(): Called by the game engine to close the player's game session. When the user decides to leave the table, the game engine has to call this service and provide all the game's session parameters. This service also has to be called automatically for every participant when a table ends, either because there are too few participants or because it has been manually ended by an operator (see Figure 6-6).

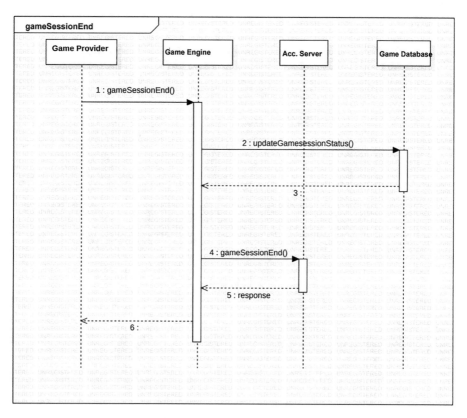

Figure 6-6. *Game session end*

7. tableEnd(): Called by the game engine to close
    the table. A game table ends at a specified time,
    when there are too few participants in a period,
    or when the table is manually closed through the
    administration tool. The table cannot be closed in
    the middle of a hand; the game engine waits for the
    current hand to finish before closing the table. In
    any case, the message must be sent after the last
    GameSessionEnd. If a GameSessionEnd has timed
    out (after all the retries), it will be possible to send
    TableEnd before it (see Figure 6-7).

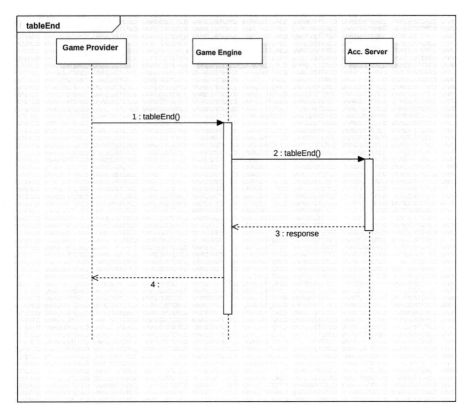

Figure 6-7. Table end

8.   addFunds(): Called by the game engine before
     moving more money from the customer's e-wallet to
     the table. The add funds request is generated by the
     user on the client side after clicking the Add Funds
     button (see Figure 6-8).

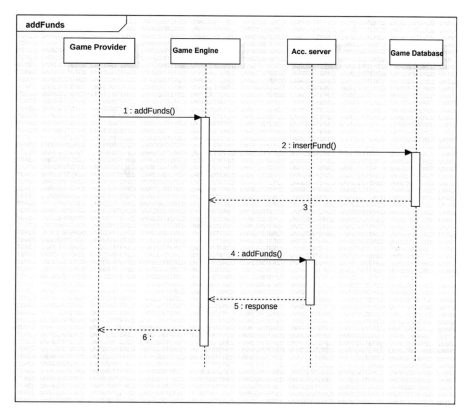

Figure 6-8. Add funds

9. addFundsCancellation(): Called by the game
    engine every time a request to add funds must be
    cancelled. The engine has to call this service every
    time there is a problem with the AddFunds API call
    (see Figure 6-9).

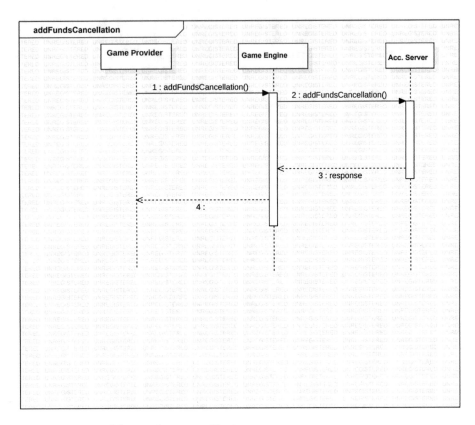

Figure 6-9. *Add Funds Cancellation*

10.   addBonus(): Called by the game engine every time there's a request to add a bonus. The game engine has to call this service every time there is a credit to a user's game account (see Figure 6-10).

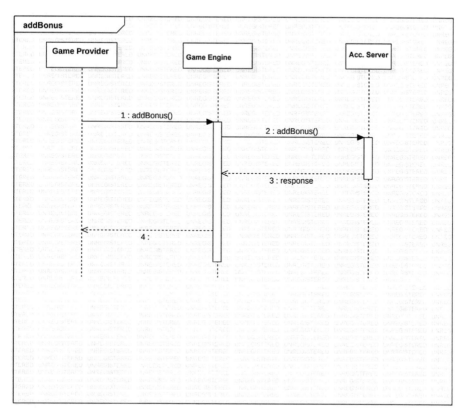

Figure 6-10. *Add bonus*

11. userLogOff(): Called by the game engine to invalidate the token. When the user logs off the game client, the game engine will call the UserLogoff service provided by game's provider network interface. For this service, the game provider network interface acts as a proxy toward the operators (see Figure 6-11).

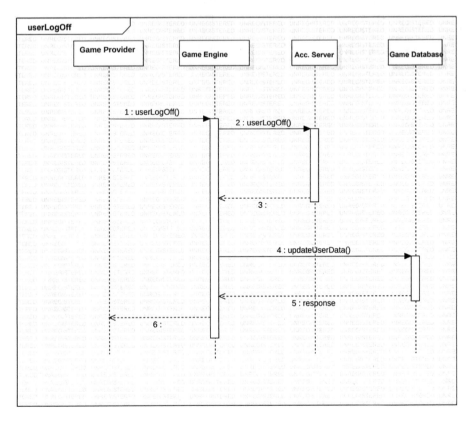

Figure 6-11. *User Log Off*

General Description of the Game's Services

Table 6-2 contains a list of all the services provided through their interface mechanism.

Table 6-2. *List of Services and the Interface Mechanism*

Service Name	Service Type	Synchronous/ Asynchronous
Table Registration	Web service over HTTP WS-I Basic Profile 1.0	Synchronous Call
Game Session Start	Web service over HTTP WS-I Basic Profile 1.0	Synchronous Call
Add Funds	Web service over HTTP WS-I Basic Profile 1.0	Synchronous Call
Add Funds Cancellation	Web service over HTTP WS-I Basic Profile 1.0	Synchronous Call
Add Bonus	Web service over HTTP WS-I Basic Profile 1.0	Synchronous Call
Game Session End	Web service over HTTP WS-I Basic Profile 1.0	Synchronous Call
Table End	Web service over HTTP WS-I Basic Profile 1.0	Synchronous Call
User Authentication	Web service over HTTP WS-I Basic Profile 1.0	Synchronous Call
Verify Token	Web service over HTTP WS-I Basic Profile 1.0	Synchronous Call
User Balance	Web service over HTTP WS-I Basic Profile 1.0	Synchronous Call
User LogOff	Web service over HTTP WS-I Basic Profile 1.0	Synchronous Call

Figure 6-12 depicts the game's general design from frontend and backend perspectives with the following five scenarios:

189

1. **Game launch:** The player clicks on the Game icon via the web portal to launch the specific game. Then, with the help of the game service, the web portal creates an SSO token. To create an SSO token, the calling system will be the token generation server. Then cashier module asks for the open game sessions from the game provider. The cashier calls the getOpenSession with the following:

Inputs

1. userId

2. productid

3. platformId

4. gameId

Outputs

1. activeSession

2. openSessions

3. latestSessions

2. **Cashier opened:** The player selects the buyin amount and clicks on the game via the web portal. The cashier module then sends the buyin amount to the provider and launches the game on the external game platform by passing the SSO Token. The "Buyin Mode Interface Component" provides to the EGP all services needed to manage game events and provides the player's information like the balance. It has following services:

- Direct purchase services

- Account services

- Cashier services

a. The cashier verifies the SSO token against the
   game provider, then starts the game session and
   gets the player balance (using the account service
   "Buyin Mode Interface Component"). Once the
   game is loaded, the EGP sends a «GameInitDone»
   message to the cashier component and the game
   is shown to the player.

b. The Game Session ID is shown to the player via
   the game frontend system.

c. The account balance (buy-in amount) is shown
   to the player (using the Account service "Buyin
   Mode Interface Component").

3. **Game open:** The player clicks on the game spin
   button, the cashier sends a «SpinStarted» message
   to the cashier module, and the cashier sends a
   PlayerPurchase to the game provider. The reels
   start spinning. Once the spin is complete, the game
   engine the sends a game round end to the game
   provider and it sends a «SpinStopped» message to
   the cashier module. The reel stops spinning .

   a. If the player wins, the winning animation
      is shown on the game. The two types
      of transactions using FundAmountVO[ ]
      typologies are:

      1. RM if the win amount is in real money

      2. FF if the win amount is in virtual money

   b. The player's account balance (buy-in amount)
      is refreshed after each spin (using the Account
      service of "Buyin Mode Interface Component").

4. **Cashier open:** If a player adds money, the cashier module sends an addFunds to the game provider. The cashier services of "Buyin Mode Interface Component" will be called and will update the balance. When a player changes their balance, it indicates that A has to call the playerBalance backend service to update amount.

5. **Game close:** Finally, the player clicks on the Exit button to close the game. The cashier module sends a BuyOut to the game provider. It then calls closeGame on the cashier, and the cashier sends a game session end to the game provider and closes the game. It sends an «GameCloseDone» message to the cashier module.

   a. BuyOut: The cashier will call the Buyout service provided by the "Buyin Mode Interface" to close the game session. For each request, the system will respond with a result code and result description.

   b. closeGame: This event is sent from the provider to the cashier. It's sent when a player clicks on the Close button in the provider cashier. It indicates that EGP has to close the game session and invoke the GameSessionEnd service on the backend side.

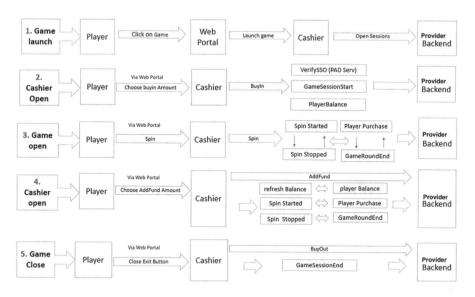

Figure 6-12. *Game's general design from frontend and backend perspectives*

Network Interfaces and Sequence Diagram for the Game Development Cycle

Games use user interface features that combine established patterns with the game's story. User interface design includes a fictional aspect when applied to games. In the fiction, an avatar of the actual user, or player, appears.

The player, like a narrator in a narrative or film, becomes an unnoticed but essential part of the plot. This fiction might be directly related to the UI, indirectly related, or not related at all. Traditionally, games had no significant connection to a storyline, most likely because early games lacked gripping storyline aspects.

In this section, we review the overall network interfaces of the game and its Web Services Description Language (WSDL). We also look at the sequence diagrams for game development.

Game Network Interfaces

An interface has a simple syntax that is similar to a class specification. It allows you to describe the high-level functionality for a certain feature, such as interaction. An interface only allows you to specify functionality, not execute it. For example, you declare the signatures of a function but not its body. An interface is a contract that exists between a class and the player.

This means that the compiler will need you to execute the body of each method declared on the interface. Several interfaces can be used to extend a class. The interfaces can be represented in the form of web services. These web services can be represented with the help of WSDL.

WSDL specifies the location and methods of the service. Listing 6-1 is written in plain XML so that the file can be read by any programming language.

The WSDLs are broken down into sections:

- **Section 1:** Describes the table registration of the game for the player. The following parameters are involved in table registration: userId, playerId, tableId, and so on. Once the table has been built, the following step is to add money to the table for the game.

- **Section 2:** Describes how to add funds to the game's table. The following factors are included in AddFunds: add fund, jackpot, bonus, withdrawal, etc. Once the fund has been added, the next step is to verify the token for the transaction.

- **Section 3:** In the general table, addFunds requires token verification. This transaction requires two types of verification: general taken verification and SSO (single signed token) token verification.

- **Section 4:** During this section, the player's balance will be displayed as well as the amount saved in the player's wallet. These transactions will be recorded in this section.

- **Section 5:** This is the final stage, and the user will be logged out.

Listing 6-1. WSDL for Game Development

```
Section 1:
<?xml version="1.0" encoding="UTF-8"?>
<definitions name='GameServiceWS' targetNamespace='http://
providerwebsite.com/game' xmlns='http://schemas.xmlsoap.
org/wsdl/' xmlns:ns1='http://beans.game.ltm.com/types'
xmlns:ns2='http://beans.game.ltm.com/jaws' xmlns:soap='http://
schemas.xmlsoap.org/wsdl/soap/' xmlns:tns='http://
providerwebsite.com/game' xmlns:xsd='http://www.w3.org/2001/
XMLSchema'>
 <types>
  <schema targetNamespace='http://beans.game.ltm.com/types'
  xmlns='http://www.w3.org/2001/XMLSchema' xmlns:ns2='http://
  beans.game.ltm.com/jaws' xmlns:soap11-enc='http://schemas.
  xmlsoap.org/soap/encoding/' xmlns:tns='http://beans.game.
  ltm.com/types' xmlns:xsi='http://www.w3.org/2001/XMLSchema-
  instance'>
   <import namespace='http://beans.game.ltm.com/jaws'/>
   <complexType name='AddFundsCancellationInVO'>
    <sequence>
     <element name='base' nillable='true'
     type='ns2:BaseInputVO'/>
     <element name='operatorID' nillable='true' type='string'/>
     <element name='retryCounter' nillable='true' type='string'/>
```

195

```
  <element name='tableID' nillable='true' type='string'/>
  <element name='transactionID' nillable='true'
  type='string'/>
  <element name='userId' nillable='true' type='string'/>
 </sequence>
</complexType>
<complexType name='AddFundsInVO'>
 <sequence>
  <element name='base' nillable='true'
  type='ns2:BaseInputVO'/>
  <element name='bonus' nillable='true' type='string'/>
  <element name='buyIn' nillable='true' type='string'/>
  <element name='ipAddress' nillable='true' type='string'/>
  <element name='operatorID' nillable='true' type='string'/>
  <element name='phaseId' nillable='true' type='string'/>
  <element name='playBonus' nillable='true' type='string'/>
  <element name='retryCounter' nillable='true'
  type='string'/>
  <element name='tableID' nillable='true' type='string'/>
  <element name='transactionID' nillable='true'
  type='string'/>
  <element name='userId' nillable='true' type='string'/>
 </sequence>
</complexType>
<complexType name='AddFundsOutVO'>
 <complexContent>
  <extension base='tns:CommonOutVO'>
   <sequence>
    <element name='errorMessageToCustomer' nillable='true'
    type='string'/>
    <element name='idTicket' nillable='true' type='string'/>
```

```
      </sequence>
     </extension>
    </complexContent>
   </complexType>
   <complexType name='CommonOutVO'>
    <complexContent>
     <extension base='ns2:BaseOutVO'>
      <sequence>
       <element name='signatureOut' nillable='true'
       type='string'/>
       <element name='signedDataOut' nillable='true'
       type='string'/>
      </sequence>
     </extension>
    </complexContent>
   </complexType>
   <complexType name='GameSessionEndInVO'>
```

Section 2:

```
<sequence>
     <element name='base' nillable='true'
     type='ns2:BaseInputVO'/>
     <element name='buyOutPlayBonus' nillable='true'
     type='string'/>
     <element name='buyOutRealBonus' nillable='true'
     type='string'/>
     <element name='endTimeStamp' nillable='true'
     type='string'/>
     <element name='jackpotAdditionalWin' nillable='true'
     type='string'/>
     <element name='jackpotContribution' nillable='true'
     type='string'/>
```

```
    <element name='jackpotInternalWin' nillable='true'
    type='string'/>
    <element name='nrBets' nillable='true' type='string'/>
    <element name='nrPlayedHands' nillable='true'
    type='string'/>
    <element name='nrRakedHands' nillable='true'
    type='string'/>
    <element name='operatorID' nillable='true' type='string'/>
    <element name='phaseId' nillable='true' type='string'/>
    <element name='retryCounter' nillable='true'
    type='string'/>
    <element name='returnedPlayBonus' nillable='true'
    type='string'/>
    <element name='returnedRealBonus' nillable='true'
    type='string'/>
    <element name='tableID' nillable='true' type='string'/>
    <element name='totalBuyIn' nillable='true' type='string'/>
    <element name='totalRake' nillable='true' type='string'/>
    <element name='totalWager' nillable='true' type='string'/>
    <element name='totalWin' nillable='true' type='string'/>
    <element name='transactionID' nillable='true'
    type='string'/>
    <element name='userID' nillable='true' type='string'/>
    <element name='wagerPlayBonus' nillable='true'
    type='string'/>
    <element name='wagerRealBonus' nillable='true'
    type='string'/>
  </sequence>
 </complexType>
 <complexType name='GameSessionStartInVO'>
  <sequence>
```

```
  <element name='IPAddress' nillable='true' type='string'/>
  <element name='base' nillable='true'
  type='ns2:BaseInputVO'/>
  <element name='bonus' nillable='true' type='string'/>
  <element name='buyIn' nillable='true' type='string'/>
  <element name='operatorID' nillable='true' type='string'/>
  <element name='phaseId' nillable='true' type='string'/>
  <element name='playBonus' nillable='true' type='string'/>
  <element name='retryCounter' nillable='true'
  type='string'/>
  <element name='startTimestamp' nillable='true'
  type='string'/>
  <element name='tableID' nillable='true' type='string'/>
  <element name='transactionID' nillable='true'
  type='string'/>
  <element name='userID' nillable='true' type='string'/>
 </sequence>
</complexType>
<complexType name='GameSessionStartOutVO'>
 <complexContent>
  <extension base='tns:CommonOutVO'>
   <sequence>
    <element name='errorMessageToCustomer' nillable='true'
    type='string'/>
    <element name='idTicket' nillable='true' type='string'/>
   </sequence>
  </extension>
 </complexContent>
</complexType>
<complexType name='TableEndInVO'>
 <sequence>
```

```
    <element name='base' nillable='true'
    type='ns2:BaseInputVO'/>
    <element name='endTimestamp' nillable='true'
    type='string'/>
    <element name='nrGameSessions' nillable='true'
    type='string'/>
    <element name='tableID' nillable='true' type='string'/>
    <element name='tableOwnerOperatorID' nillable='true'
    type='string'/>
    <element name='tablelogEndChecksum' nillable='true'
    type='string'/>
    <element name='totalRake' nillable='true' type='string'/>
    <element name='totalWager' nillable='true' type='string'/>
    <element name='totalWin' nillable='true' type='string'/>
   </sequence>
  </complexType>
  <complexType name='TableRegistrationInVO'>
   <sequence>
    <element name='ante' nillable='true' type='string'/>
    <element name='base' nillable='true'
    type='ns2:BaseInputVO'/>
    <element name='bigBlind' nillable='true' type='string'/>
<element name='bonusFlag' nillable='true' type='string'/>
    <element name='gameCode' nillable='true' type='string'/>
    <element name='jackpotAdditional' nillable='true'
    type='string'/>
    <element name='jackpotInternal' nillable='true'
    type='string'/>
    <element name='jackpotPercentage' nillable='true'
    type='string'/>
    <element name='limitType' nillable='true' type='string'/>
```

```
  <element name='maxBuyin' nillable='true' type='string'/>
  <element name='maxDuration' nillable='true'
  type='string'/>
  <element name='maxRake' nillable='true' type='string'/>
  <element name='maxRakePercentage' nillable='true'
  type='string'/>
  <element name='maxSeats' nillable='true' type='string'/>
  <element name='minBet' nillable='true' type='string'/>
  <element name='minBuyin' nillable='true' type='string'/>
  <element name='tableID' nillable='true' type='string'/>
  <element name='tableLogStartChecksum' nillable='true'
  type='string'/>
  <element name='tableName' nillable='true' type='string'/>
  <element name='tableOwnerOperatorID' nillable='true'
  type='string'/>
 </sequence>
</complexType>
<complexType name='TableRegistrationOutVO'>
 <complexContent>
  <extension base='tns:CommonOutVO'>
   <sequence>
    <element name='sessionId' nillable='true'
    type='string'/>
   </sequence>
  </extension>
 </complexContent>
</complexType>
<complexType name='UserAuthenticationInVO'>
 <sequence>
  <element name='base' nillable='true'
  type='ns2:BaseInputVO'/>
```

```
      <element name='ipAddress' nillable='true' type='string'/>
      <element name='operatorID' nillable='true' type='string'/>
      <element name='password' nillable='true' type='string'/>
      <element name='username' nillable='true' type='string'/>
    </sequence>
  </complexType>
  <complexType name='UserAuthenticationOutVO'>
   <complexContent>
    <extension base='tns:CommonOutVO'>
     <sequence>
      <element name='networkNickname' nillable='true'
      type='string'/>
      <element name='token' nillable='true' type='string'/>
      <element name='userID' nillable='true' type='string'/>
     </sequence>
    </extension>
   </complexContent>
  </complexType>
  <complexType name='UserBalanceInVO'>
   <sequence>
    <element name='base' nillable='true'
    type='ns2:BaseInputVO'/>
    <element name='operatorID' nillable='true' type='string'/>
    <element name='userID' nillable='true' type='string'/>
   </sequence>
  </complexType>
  <complexType name='UserBalanceOutVO'>
   <complexContent>
    <extension base='tns:CommonOutVO'>
     <sequence>
      <element name='userBalance' nillable='true' type='string'/>
```

```
    </sequence>
   </extension>
  </complexContent>
 </complexType>
 <complexType name='UserLogOffInVO'>
  <sequence>
   <element name='base' nillable='true' type='ns2:BaseInputVO'/>
   <element name='operatorID' nillable='true' type='string'/>
   <element name='token' nillable='true' type='string'/>
   <element name='userID' nillable='true' type='string'/>
  </sequence>
```

Section 3:

```
  </complexType>
  <complexType name='VerifyTokenInVO'>
   <sequence>
    <element name='base' nillable='true'
    type='ns2:BaseInputVO'/>
    <element name='operatorID' nillable='true' type='string'/>
    <element name='token' nillable='true' type='string'/>
    <element name='userID' nillable='true' type='string'/>
   </sequence>
  </complexType>
  <complexType name='VerifyTokenOutVO'>
   <complexContent>
    <extension base='tns:CommonOutVO'>
     <sequence>
      <element name='networkNickname' nillable='true'
      type='string'/>
     </sequence>
    </extension>
   </complexContent>
```

```
   </complexType>
  </schema>
  <schema targetNamespace='http://beans.game.ltm.com/jaws'
  xmlns='http://www.w3.org/2001/XMLSchema' xmlns:ns1='http://
  beans.game.ltm.com/types' xmlns:soap11-enc='http://schemas.
  xmlsoap.org/soap/encoding/' xmlns:tns='http://beans.game.
  ltm.com/jaws' xmlns:xsi='http://www.w3.org/2001/XMLSchema-
  instance'>
   <import namespace='http://beans.game.ltm.com/types'/>
   <complexType name='BaseInputVO'>
    <sequence>
     <element name='signatureIn' nillable='true'
     type='string'/>
     <element name='signedDataIn' nillable='true'
     type='string'/>
    </sequence>
   </complexType>
   <complexType name='BaseOutVO'>
    <sequence>
     <element name='resultCode' nillable='true' type='string'/>
     <element name='resultDesc' nillable='true' type='string'/>
    </sequence>
   </complexType>
  </schema>
 </types>
 <message name='GameServiceWS_addFunds'>
  <part name='AddFundsInVO_1' type='ns1:AddFundsInVO'/>
 </message>
 <message name='GameServiceWS_addFundsResponse'>
  <part name='result' type='ns1:AddFundsOutVO'/>
 </message>
```

```
<message name='GameServiceWS_addFundsCancellation'>
 <part name='AddFundsCancellationInVO_1' type='ns1:AddFundsCan
 cellationInVO'/>
</message>
<message name='GameServiceWS_addFundsCancellationResponse'>
 <part name='result' type='ns1:CommonOutVO'/>
</message>
<message name='GameServiceWS_gameSessionEnd'>
 <part name='GameSessionEndInVO_1' type='ns1:GameSession
 EndInVO'/>
</message>
<message name='GameServiceWS_gameSessionEndResponse'>
 <part name='result' type='ns1:CommonOutVO'/>
</message>
<message name='GameServiceWS_gameSessionStart'>
 <part name='GameSessionStartInVO_1' type='ns1:GameSession
 StartInVO'/>
</message>
<message name='GameServiceWS_gameSessionStartResponse'>
 <part name='result' type='ns1:GameSessionStartOutVO'/>
</message>
<message name='GameServiceWS_tableEnd'>
 <part name='TableEndInVO_1' type='ns1:TableEndInVO'/>
</message>
<message name='GameServiceWS_tableEndResponse'>
 <part name='result' type='ns1:CommonOutVO'/>
</message>
<message name='GameServiceWS_tableRegistration'>
 <part name='TableRegistrationInVO_1' type='ns1:
 TableRegistrationInVO'/>
```

Section 4:

```
</message>
 <message name='GameServiceWS_tableRegistrationResponse'>
  <part name='result' type='ns1:TableRegistrationOutVO'/>
 </message>
 <message name='GameServiceWS_userAuthentication'>
  <part name='UserAuthenticationInVO_1' type='ns1:
  UserAuthenticationInVO'/>
 </message>
 <message name='GameServiceWS_userAuthenticationResponse'>
  <part name='result' type='ns1:UserAuthenticationOutVO'/>
 </message>
 <message name='GameServiceWS_userBalance'>
  <part name='UserBalanceInVO_1' type='ns1:UserBalanceInVO'/>
 </message>
 <message name='GameServiceWS_userBalanceResponse'>
  <part name='result' type='ns1:UserBalanceOutVO'/>
 </message>
 <message name='GameServiceWS_userLogOff'>
  <part name='UserLogOffInVO_1' type='ns1:UserLogOffInVO'/>
 </message>
 <message name='GameServiceWS_userLogOffResponse'>
  <part name='result' type='ns1:CommonOutVO'/>
 </message>
 <message name='GameServiceWS_verifyToken'>
  <part name='VerifyTokenInVO_1' type='ns1:VerifyTokenInVO'/>
 </message>
 <message name='GameServiceWS_verifyTokenResponse'>
  <part name='result' type='ns1:VerifyTokenOutVO'/>
 </message>
 <portType name='GameServiceWS'>
```

```
<operation name='addFunds' parameterOrder='AddFundsInVO_1'>
 <input message='tns:GameServiceWS_addFunds'/>
 <output message='tns:GameServiceWS_addFundsResponse'/>
</operation>
<operation name='addFundsCancellation' parameterOrder=
'AddFundsCancellationInVO_1'>
 <input message='tns:GameServiceWS_addFundsCancellation'/>
 <output message='tns:GameServiceWS_addFundsCancellation
 Response'/>
</operation>
<operation name='gameSessionEnd' parameterOrder=
'GameSessionEndInVO_1'>
 <input message='tns:GameServiceWS_gameSessionEnd'/>
 <output message='tns:GameServiceWS_gameSessionEndResponse'/>
</operation>
<operation name='gameSessionStart' parameterOrder=
'GameSessionStartInVO_1'>
 <input message='tns:GameServiceWS_gameSessionStart'/>
 <output message='tns:GameServiceWS_gameSessionStart
 Response'/>
</operation>
<operation name='tableEnd' parameterOrder='TableEndInVO_1'>
 <input message='tns:GameServiceWS_tableEnd'/>
 <output message='tns:GameServiceWS_tableEndResponse'/>
</operation>
<operation name='tableRegistration' parameterOrder=
'TableRegistrationInVO_1'>
 <input message='tns:GameServiceWS_tableRegistration'/>
 <output message='tns:GameServiceWS_tableRegistration
 Response'/>
</operation>
```

```
<operation name='userAuthentication' parameterOrder=
'UserAuthenticationInVO_1'>
 <input message='tns:GameServiceWS_userAuthentication'/>
 <output message='tns:GameServiceWS_userAuthentication
 Response'/>
</operation>
<operation name='userBalance' parameterOrder=
'UserBalanceInVO_1'>
 <input message='tns:GameServiceWS_userBalance'/>
 <output message='tns:GameServiceWS_userBalanceResponse'/>
</operation>
<operation name='userLogOff' parameterOrder='UserLogOff
InVO_1'>
 <input message='tns:GameServiceWS_userLogOff'/>
 <output message='tns:GameServiceWS_userLogOffResponse'/>
</operation>
<operation name='verifyToken' parameterOrder='Verify
TokenInVO_1'>
 <input message='tns:GameServiceWS_verifyToken'/>
 <output message='tns:GameServiceWS_verifyTokenResponse'/>
</operation>
</portType>
<binding name='GameServiceWSBinding' type='tns:GameServiceWS'>
<soap:binding style='rpc' transport='http://schemas.xmlsoap.
org/soap/http'/>
 <operation name='addFunds'>
  <soap:operation soapAction=''/>
  <input>
   <soap:body namespace='http://providerwebsite.com/game'
   use='literal'/>
  </input>
  <output>
```

```
  <soap:body namespace='http://providerwebsite.com/game'
  use='literal'/>
 </output>
</operation>
<operation name='addFundsCancellation'>
 <soap:operation soapAction=''/>
 <input>
  <soap:body namespace='http://providerwebsite.com/game'
  use='literal'/>
 </input>
 <output>
  <soap:body namespace='http://providerwebsite.com/game'
  use='literal'/>
 </output>
</operation>
<operation name='gameSessionEnd'>
 <soap:operation soapAction=''/>
 <input>
  <soap:body namespace='http://providerwebsite.com/game'
  use='literal'/>
 </input>
 <output>
  <soap:body namespace='http://providerwebsite.com/game'
  use='literal'/>
 </output>
</operation>
<operation name='gameSessionStart'>
 <soap:operation soapAction=''/>
 <input>
  <soap:body namespace='http://providerwebsite.com/game'
  use='literal'/>
```

```
   </input>
   <output>
    <soap:body namespace='http://providerwebsite.com/game'
    use='literal'/>
   </output>
  </operation>
  <operation name='tableEnd'>
   <soap:operation soapAction=''/>
   <input>
    <soap:body namespace='http://providerwebsite.com/game'
    use='literal'/>
   </input>
   <output>
    <soap:body namespace='http://providerwebsite.com/game'
    use='literal'/>
   </output>

Section 5:
 </operation>
  <operation name='tableRegistration'>
   <soap:operation soapAction=''/>
   <input>
    <soap:body namespace='http://providerwebsite.com/game'
    use='literal'/>
   </input>
   <output>
    <soap:body namespace='http://providerwebsite.com/game'
    use='literal'/>
   </output>
  </operation>
  <operation name='userAuthentication'>
   <soap:operation soapAction=''/>
```

```
 <input>
  <soap:body namespace='http://providerwebsite.com/game'
  use='literal'/>
 </input>
 <output>
  <soap:body namespace='http://providerwebsite.com/game'
  use='literal'/>
 </output>
</operation>
<operation name='userBalance'>
 <soap:operation soapAction=''/>
 <input>
  <soap:body namespace='http://providerwebsite.com/game'
  use='literal'/>
 </input>
 <output>
  <soap:body namespace='http://providerwebsite.com/game'
  use='literal'/>
 </output>
</operation>
<operation name='userLogOff'>
 <soap:operation soapAction=''/>
 <input>
  <soap:body namespace='http://providerwebsite.com/game'
  use='literal'/>
 </input>
 <output>
  <soap:body namespace='http://providerwebsite.com/game'
  use='literal'/>
 </output>
</operation>
```

```
  <operation name='verifyToken'>
   <soap:operation soapAction=''/>
   <input>
    <soap:body namespace='http://providerwebsite.com/game'
    use='literal'/>
   </input>
   <output>
    <soap:body namespace='http://providerwebsite.com/game'
    use='literal'/>
   </output>
  </operation>
 </binding>
 <service name='GameServiceWS'>
  <port binding='tns:GameServiceWSBinding'
  name='GameServiceWSPort'>
   <soap:address location='REPLACE_WITH_ACTUAL_URL'/>
  </port>
 </service>
</definitions>
```

The preceding WSDL provides you with several services that are
needed in the game architecture. The next section explores the sequence
diagram used to represent these services.

Sequence Diagrams

We'll go over sequence diagrams for the cash table, game launch, and
tournament in this section (Figures 6-13 through 6-15). These sequence
diagrams can be used to create games for two popular areas: casinos and
tournaments.

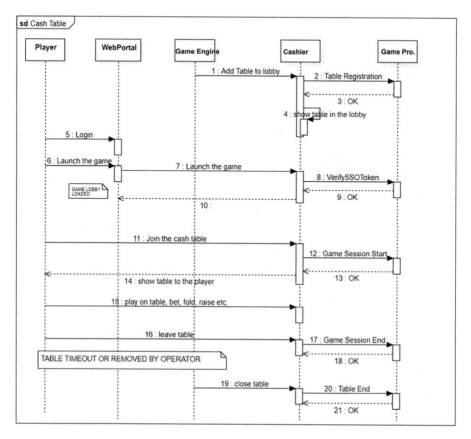

Figure 6-13. *Cash table*

Each diagram depicts the input and output values that are taken into account during the game cycle. Each component's transaction is processed by the game engine, while the fund-related section is handled by the cashier. The user can engage through the online portal. The registration for the table will be kept in the cashier area.

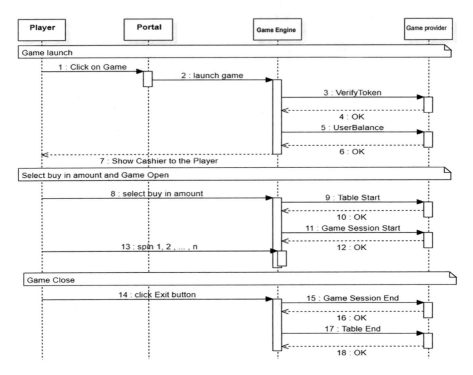

Figure 6-14. Game launch

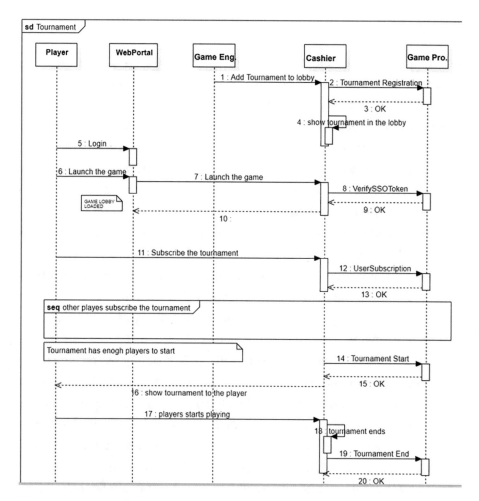

Figure 6-15. *Tournament*

In the development cycle, the majority of online games (casino or tournament) employ the same pattern or design. Let's look at them now.

Casino Games

Gambling sites are virtual versions of land-based casinos. They're also referred to as online casinos or virtual casinos. Online casinos allow gamblers to play and wager on casino games over the Internet. It is a widely used form of Internet gaming. Games are played in a casino website in the same way they are at a real casino. The main distinction is that online casino games rely on computer-generated randomization, whereas real-world casinos have a person on the other side of the table.

Streaming online gaming, contrary to several of the technologies that have transformed the history of online casinos, is a gaming experience that is partly online (hence only available on the fastest platforms, such as digital) and partially "live." This is largely facilitated by the fact that the platform to which you connect has a window that looks out onto a genuine casino, where you may play, gamble, and win just like you would if you were actually inside one.

It's essentially a broadcast station with a live croupier overseeing the game's activities and numerous wagers. These are not actors, but real and qualified croupiers who have gone through a rigorous training program in order to do this task. Essentially, they're the same ones you'd find in a real casino. In certain situations, it is the ground casinos itself that lend their rooms to the licensing of the online platforms, broadcasting live without pausing their croupiers and tables, who have the responsibility of fulfilling the bets according to the orders, 24 hours a day, without interruption. Those who play from home will eventually take on the role of croupier, pulling the ball if they're in front of a roulette wheel or dealing the cards if they're at a poker table.

There are various advantages to using digital platforms' "Live Casino" sections. First and foremost, the travel, with significant time and money savings. Instead of long delays on the highway or at the airport, it just takes a few seconds to be hurled into the gaming area, near the green tables. Another advantage is the ability to communicate with the croupier and other players via chat: you welcome, discuss, and potentially take all required measures. Not only that, but in addition to the replies from the croupiers, you can hear the characteristic sounds of casinos, such as slots spinning or roulette balls halting within the renowned metal cylinder. Many times, at a genuine casino, only one table is open and there is a large throng waiting to play the game you want. The live connection, on the other hand, has a virtually infinite supply of seats: you will nearly never have to wait. The other undeniable advantage is the feeling that playing in live mode gives those who participate in the sessions.

The odds of winning are the same, but the benefit of a live casino is exactly in watching the ball literally travel between the boxes during live roulette games, which gives players a sense of realism that is tough to reproduce with software. Last but not least, one of the clear advantages of live online casinos over land-based casinos is the ability to play in your jammies or as you choose. There are no dress requirements to follow.

Tournament Games

A tournament is a contest in which at least three people compete in the same sport or game. More exactly, the phrase can be interpreted in one of two ways: A competition or series of contests held in a single location over a short period of time. Figure 6-16 shows a 16-player single elimination tournament: 12 games have been played, and the winner of Lisa/Ernie will play the winner of Andrew/Robert in the final.

Figure 6-16.   Tournament players

Table registration for tournament games differs differently from that of casino games. As you can see from the table in Figure 6-16, the event will include extra tables in the gaming sessions.

Security of Online Games Through a Web Portal

When we develop games, we need to use a "secure" game development process, during all phases of the Development Life Cycle (SDLC) through the identification and implementation of appropriate safety. SDLC is a process used to develop and manage software efficiently in order to improve the quality of the software produced and to ensure that it achieves the objectives for which it was created. The issue is so relevant that it has been included in an International Organization for Standardization. When it comes to secure game creation, the following factors must be addressed.

Security in all phases of the software development cycle: an in-depth examination of the various SDLC phases to underline the need of considering security concerns from the start of the SDLC.

To overcome the present security issues caused by design and/or implementation flaws, training and education are required. Only skilled and knowledgeable personnel can fix the difficulties.

Secure Code for Games

The guidelines presented constitute a set of best practices to be followed in order to prevent security problems in the code, and at the same time provide a useful tool in identifying possible vulnerabilities in the source code and the related countermeasures to be applied. The recommended approach depends on the type of project. In the case of designing applications from scratch, a secure by design approach is suggested, while in the case of re-engineering existing applications, the adoption of a security control approach is recommended.

In any case, you need to avoid insecure code. A basic illustration of what it takes for an attacker to accomplish a buffer overrun attack is as follows[1]:

---

[1] https://docs.microsoft.com/en-us/windows/win32/dxtecharts/best-security-practices-in-game-development

```
void GetPlayerName(char *pDatafromNet)
{
    char playername[256];
    strncpy(playername, pDatafromNet, strlen(pDatafromNet));

    // ...
}
```

On the surface, this code appears to be correct; after all, it calls a safe function. Data from the network is copied into a 256-byte buffer. The strncpy function is either restricted by the specified buffer count or relies on detecting a NULL terminator in the source string[1].

The buffer size is wrong, which is the issue. If network data isn't verified or if the buffer size is incorrect (as in this case), an attacker might simply give a huge buffer and replace stack data with whatever data in the network packet after the buffer ends. By rewriting the instruction pointer and modifying the return address, the attacker might execute arbitrary code. The most fundamental takeaway from this example is that input should never be trusted unless it has been checked[1].

Even if the data does not originate from the networks, there is still a danger. Many individuals must design, create, and test the same code base in modern game development. It's impossible to predict how the function will be used in the future[1].

Secure by Design

During the application security analysis phases of a system architecture, it is necessary to implement safe design practices through the identification of security requirements and countermeasures according to the security by design principles. Secure design practices realize information security through a "defense in depth" approach of the application layer. The "defense in depth" approach aims to minimize damage in the event of a successful attack. In practice, if an attacker manages to overcome the first level of defense, more restrictive measures must intervene to hinder its advance. (For example, by restricting access privileges to a minimum to resources or by applying application compartmentalization in order to block the propagation of the attack to the entire system.)

Security Control

If you are making changes to an existing application, you need to keep the following points in mind:

- Identify, quantify, and resolve the security risks associated with an existing interface, application, and/or system.

- Validate from the point of view of application security the developments made by third parties (supply chain security).

- Protect their information assets and data.

Creating a game for today's and tomorrow's markets is both expensive and time-consuming. Putting out a game with security flaws will end up costing more money and effort to correct. As a result, it is in all game makers' best interests to incorporate tools and procedures to remediate security flaws prior to release.

Summary

In the gaming sector, each provider creates a game with proprietary technology. In this chapter, you learned how to create a comprehensive design and architecture for game development. You were able to see the generic patterns in game design. You could use this same methodology in game development with any programming language. The methodology of gamification is discussed in the next chapter.

CHAPTER 7

Gamification in Human-Computer Interaction

This chapter explores gamification in HCI. Because gamification has been shown to increase the effectiveness of educational processes, creativity, enjoyment, productivity, and the capacity to retain knowledge and gain new abilities, it is the principal objective style of game development. The use of thinking and gaming approaches in non-entertainment environments, such as education and labor, is referred to as the HCI approach.

This chapter also covers common gamification risks and pitfalls, as well as factors that make gamification in the classroom easier. Gamification has a plethora of applications, and this chapter touches on a few of them, as well as its applications in game development.

© Joseph Thachil George, Meghna Joseph George 2022
J. T. George and M. J. George, *Human-Computer Interaction in Game Development with Python*, https://doi.org/10.1007/978-1-4842-8182-6_7

Gamification Strategy

Over the years, gamification has been defined in many ways. In a nutshell, though, *gamification* is the application of game design concepts to non-game environments in order to achieve a certain aim, which is to boost user engagement.

To successfully apply gamification in sectors such as training, marketing, or human resources requires an understanding of one's potential users, who, even before being students, potential buyers, or employees of a company, are lovers of the game. Elements such as points and badges are useful basic mechanics to encourage their participation.

However, the simple act of performing particular tasks for obtaining "exclusive" points or badges does not offer any meaningful interaction to the player, who will seek to behave and think according to the choices that they must make to achieve the game's primary reward. To create real engagement, you need to develop consistent and meaningful gaming experiences, using the combination of game elements best suited to the objectives you want to pursue. If the strategy is limited to inserting points or badges only, without a precise idea of what you want the user to gain from the experience, the results will be poor, offering little value for the user and increasing the likelihood they will simply give up.

Gamification seeks to reconcile the goals of the player with the goals of the game designer. As an example, the famous *Super Mario* has recently incorporated a smartwatch from a well-known Californian company into its game system. The watch has game mechanics and uses gamification.

- Mario's goal is to exercise and stay fit.

- The company's goal is to make the use of the product a routine and then sell straps and a monthly plan with personalized exercises.

In this example, gamification is used to encourage physical activity through the device. Creating a new routine allows the company to sell straps and subscription products.

In games, people get excited, create friendships, compete, and lose track of time. In everyday life, you rarely experience the same sensations as during games. Work, school, and institutions are often not designed with people's involvement in mind.

Gamification Examples

Gamification is getting growing feedback in companies and especially in the field of education, basically because its results can be seen and in many cases are tangible.

In any case, the metaverse, in our opinion, is the pinnacle of gaming technology's application to non-game goals, akin to "gamification for real."

The employment of game elements and tactics in non-game situations is known as *gamification*. It attracts visitors by using point scoring, competition with others, and scorekeeping, among other things. Its goal is to influence the behavior of consumers who participate in the "game" and enhance engagement.

The metaverse is more than just a collection of fascinating features.

Coming up with a good concept is simple; the difficult part is putting it into practice. Virtual reality offers a lot of potential for organizations, but that potential is being overlooked due to the "careless" manner in which it is being used.

Companies tend to focus on the "virtual" to the exclusion of the "real" when it comes to metaverses and virtual reality. That is, they ignore the truth about what makes metaverses so fascinating, especially when mixed with virtual reality. This is one of the major problems with the practice.

A metaverse is a real-time rendering of physical and digital assets that fluidly overlap and combine to create a participatory and deconstructed 3D environment. Similar to patient objects and individualities, participating histories, rights/entitlements, the ability to make payments, etc., there is a sense of durability that parallels real life.

Even if a large number of people join the metaverse at the same time, each person retains their own sense of existence.

In the online journal on its site, Accenture gives a noteworthy interpretation of why gamification works so well. The potential of game-based business applications increases due to the combined effect of two major trends:

- Generation Y, the millennials, increasingly make up enthusiastic online gamers and appreciate communication methods based on games.

- Increasing crowding of the digital space, which makes it difficult for companies to get noticed and be able to communicate their message.

The best-known cases of gamification confirm that, if you guess right, the initiatives in this context they can be very rewarding.

But how can the benefits of gamification be described? What are the main advantages and on which terrains are they located? A list of benefits can be the following:

- **Fun.** If you do not neglect the essential fun ingredient, gamification can entertain, relax, and give users a good time, which is always useful for associating positive feelings toward the application, the company, or the brand.

- **Involvement.** Engagement is one of the primary goals of gamified projects and often one of their best and most easily verifiable results.

- **Motivation.** Many experiences indicate that gamification can support motivation, both within the company and at school, stimulating people to carry out otherwise boring tasks, externally supporting the willingness of users to remain in contact with the brand or discipline.

- **Loyalty.** As in the case of Starbucks, gamification can be quite effective in raising the levels of loyalty of its consumers and customers.

- **Influence.** When the game dynamics offered are appreciated, they are able to increase the capacity of the material, of the company, or of the brand to stimulate, guide, and influence its users.

- **Relevance.** A good gamification program capable of impacting lifestyles is certainly capable of paying off the material that is the most relevant brand for consumers.

- **Retention.** In the field of learning, game mechanics support the ability to absorb and retain content of any kind.

- **Learning experience.** If truly capable of entertaining, gamification can affect the entire learning experience, making it a lot fresher and more exciting.

- **Virality.** Gamified applications can be used to get people talking about a certain brand in social media, encouraging sharing specific activities that are part of the gameplay.

- **Crowdsourcing.** Especially if the games become viral, they can be used in crowdsourcing in order to draw on forms of USG (user generated content) to solve problems or find innovative and interesting solutions.

- **Data collection.** Gamification platforms usually require login via email addresses and social credentials, and this allows you to generate large amounts of data by observing what else people attracted to the game tend to do, both on the specific platform and on the web.

The advantages of gamification are therefore multiple. And it is no coincidence that an increasing number of businesses and schools are taking games more and more into consideration. Before planning and implementing them, however, it is always good to have a clear idea of everything that can go wrong and nullify the value of the investment.

Common Risks and Mistakes

Gamification is a nascent practice, and most businesses and users have little, if any, experience with it. There being no established practices, it is understandable that mistakes can be made easily. According to Werbach and Hunter, common risks and mistakes are the following:

- **Pointification and badgification:** The most popular way to take risks to lose the potential of gamification is in setting up programs that are based too much on points, badges, and rankings and not enough on the attractiveness of the experience. Scoring systems are important, but if the gamified initiatives start and end with them they won't go far. The reason is that points and rankings involve challenges that may take time and effort, but they are not interesting in themselves and are unable to hold the interest of the participants for very long. They must be seen as extrinsic motivating factors, but they must always be thinking that true motivations derive from experiences that are inherently pleasant and above all fun.

- **Legal aspects.** If not well controlled, gamification projects they can run into various problems of a legal nature. Among them are issues relating to respect for labor rights or constraints on advertising activities. In general, you can try to solve these issues through the terms of service, which must be carefully screened to avoid possible complications.

- **Privacy.** Gamification programs tend to store lots of data relating to the players. Any activity related to the game can be traced, and this information can be cross-referenced with other data regarding the ages, addresses, and transaction histories of the users. The data must be collected in full respect of the privacy protection regulations in force in the various countries.

- **Intellectual property.** The gamification system can involve all four forms of intellectual property: copyright, trademark, patents, and trade secrets. On the one hand, it is important to protect your project and its value, and on the other hand, you must be careful not to violate the intellectual property of others. For example, it is not permissible to copy a badge system from another gamified program, unless authorization has been obtained.

- **Lotteries and gambling.** There are many laws governing gambling and competitions. Each of these domains is regulated to a significant degree, but in different ways. The relative laws can enter the field of the gamification if initiatives offer rewards of appreciable monetary value. You must therefore know which regulations your game should adhere to.

- **Misleading practices.** Games that tend to deceive users may be among the cases of commercial fraud. For example, a gamified system that induces users to choose cards credit at higher interest rates just to receive virtual rewards would be problematic.

In addition to these observations, largely relating to the relationship between gamification and the laws that regulate them, it is possible to consider additional risks that can reduce the effectiveness of the games themselves. The most relevant are the following:

- **Superficial reasons.** The game must have the ability to activate significant intrinsic or noteworthy reasons in the real world. Virtual incentives that only allow you to boast online can prove to be insufficient.

- **Rewards are too quick.** At the psychological level, if the incentives are granted too soon players will have a tendency to lose interest. Rewards must be given in relation to prolonged efforts, so that, when they arrive, they are appreciated.

- **Lack of top management support.** If gamification projects are not supported by top managers, or worse still they are seen as a waste of time or confused with simple games, they have no basis on which to succeed. Top management must be fully aware of the aims and potential value of these projects.

- **Predictability.** After the initial novelty, gamification programs can become tiresome, especially if they are predictable. The way to avoid this is to create variable incentive structures, introduce elements of randomness, renew the elements of function, and update the shape and setting of the game from time to time.

- **Not sharing.** Even if there are individual games, the game is a collective experience in which exchange is essential. Be sure to give people a chance to share their excitement and success. This approach can significantly lower the motivation to play.

- **Possibility of cheating.** The construction of a gamification project must carefully preclude the possibility of cheating. If cheating happens, most players will learn that the game is not transparent, and they will lose the will to play.

As you can see, the list of risk areas is considerable, but related to the list of possible benefits, finding the correct balance is key in all circumstances. The benefits of gamification certainly outweigh the risks, which is proven by many companies and schools that today, more and more, are taking advantage of it.

For gamification to work, you need to align playful goals through interactive modalities often in the face of a reduction of cost and effort compared to alternative solutions.

At this point, it is important to make a clarification that is perhaps obvious, but nevertheless necessary: Gamification is not the solution to all problems and to all organizational challenges. In fact, it is necessary to think of the listed dimensions as real project sub-objectives. The goal is to solve the critical issues posed by each dimension in a positive and virtuous way, in order to use gamification successfully.

Gamification in Education

This section illustrates the elements of gamification in the educational environment. The principles of the game are analyzed, including the appropriate ages, what motivates pupils to play, the psychological aspects of the players, and the importance of gaming to millennials and Generation Z.

Aspects of the Game's Foundation

In the beginning of the chapter, we showed that the game involves some primary human instincts and that through the playful dimension it is possible to obtain results not obtainable with other tools. It is possible to say that each game is able to exert "power" over its players. This goal of power gives direction to the game, orients it, clarifies its purpose, and constitutes its meaning.

Humans are goal-oriented and objectives are fundamental to this. The rules shape the game and make it clear to the players how to achieve the goal, then they trace the boundaries of the play and ensure that all players are equal. The rules represent the constraints that can make the game exciting, interesting, and inspiring. Each player needs to know when they have reached their goal or when they are close to reaching it. For this reason, every game must be equipped with a feedback system, which is essential because it provides the motivation to keep playing. The feedback allows you to measure the direct impact of the commitment and can be presented as a ranking, a score, or progress bar.

An element of voluntariness is perhaps the most important. The player chooses to play, because play is a spontaneous act that responds to one very precise logic and is able to fully and consciously involve the player. Every game is first and foremost a free act. The imposed game is no longer a game. Whoever plays decides to accept the goal, the rules, and the feedback system because they know they can give up play when they want. Precisely because it is an intentional act, this helps to make it a safe and enjoyable activity.

The Different Game Categories

To more precisely define the categories of the game, reference is made to the taxonomy proposed by Deterding, Dixon, Khaled, and Nacke[1], in which the relationship between gaming and playing is explained, as shown in Figure 7-1.

---

[1] Deterding S., Meaningful Play. Getting "Gamification" Right. Presentation, Google Tech Talk, 24 Gennaio, 2011, Mountain View, California CA, http://codingconduct.cc/Meaningful-Play

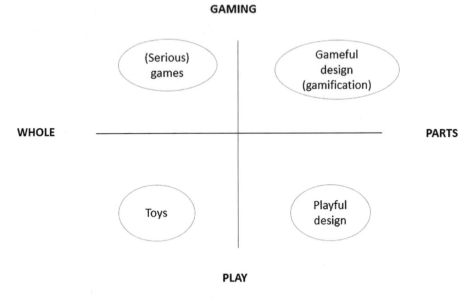

Figure 7-1. *Between the game's categories, there is a taxonomy*

If it is true that gamification is the application of elements of the game with non-playful texts, then we will place it in the upper-right quadrant called Gameful Design (gamification). When instead we are faced with real games, we find ourselves in upper-left quadrant. When the games are applied to non-playful contexts, such as a mental simulation designed with an educational purpose, they are Serious games. If you move down to left, you find Toys, which are pure video games (see Figure 7-1).

In reality, they are not games, because they have neither goals nor objectives, but they are simply made to play together. The last quadrant at the bottom right represents the Playful Design, i.e. the application of some typical playful elements of play and not of games. In English, "to play" means both to play a part and to play an instrument, while the game is an organized game. In each case, the difference between the two concepts is given by the notion of rule, structure, and scheme. Finally, it is necessary to underline that in some cases the boundaries between the classes of this taxonomy can be labile and subjective.

Psychology and Motivation in Gamification

Gamification includes a series of psychological concepts, especially in regard to motivation. Trying to master and understand these concepts becomes one of the most important keys for a correct implementation of gamification.

The main social dynamics that make gamification so effective are driven by a very strong motivational component. And gamification itself extends this component, motivating people to perform certain activities. It becomes important to understand the psychology of motivation by trying to understand the different types and how to encourage them over time, thus enriching the experience lived by the players.

The Two Different Types of Motivation

Regardless of how gamification is approached, the main classification of motivation falls into two types: intrinsic and extrinsic. Intrinsic motivation originates within the individual, rather than being generated in the surrounding world.

This derives from a situation of curiosity, genuine involvement, and the desire to increase one's own skills. People engage in a specific activity because they find it challenging, rewarding, and satisfying. Users are moved by different and subjective intrinsic motivators.

On the contrary, extrinsic motivation is generated more often than not by factors external to the user, such as the desire to receive recognition or avoid unpleasant situations. The basic concept is not so much the wanting to do something, as much as the perception of having to do it.

There is no type of motivation better than the other, while experiences in the educational field show that gamification works best when it is designed to align and integrate intrinsic motivations and extrinsic variables.

Playing and Learning

Study and fun are often seen as contradictory. This perspective remains perhaps a little dated and does not take into account the fact that a lot depends on how you study and play.

Research that investigates moments of leisure assume almost exclusively the point of view of the adult. Only recently have we come to consider the game of adolescents as an answer to the same entertainment needs, escape from reality, or building friendships. Teenage play has become a field of interest for developmental psychology, which has associated it with building their intelligence.

The genesis and development of the game for young people has been thoroughly analyzed and it is now an established fact that children learn while they play. It is on this basis that we find a union between play and learning, whatever form the game takes. Often, in fact, we accept the idea that children learn by playing, not paying enough attention to the modalities of learning in different situations. The transition from the gaming experience to content learning is in some cases very mysterious.

That play can have a much more fruitful relationship with study, where the meaning of knowledge today has shifted from being able to remember and repeat information to being able to find, evaluate, and use information in convincing way in the right context.

Education in the early part of the 20th Century tended to focus on the acquisition of basic skills and knowledge of content such as reading, writing, and mathematics. Many experts, on the other hand, believe that success in the 21st Century depends on an education that develops higher level skills, such as the ability to think, solve complex problems, and interact critically through language and media.

To cope with these contemporary challenges, the skills acquired through games are fundamental. This statement puts in relationship many of the normal teaching and learning practices and all this has already become part of the area of gamification that deals with e-learning. The use of game elements motivates students to follow the courses more carefully and supports the absorption of the contents. The game elements that can be used to motivate pupils and facilitate learning include the following points:

- Progress mechanics (points, badges, and rankings)

- Narratives; control of the player

- Immediate feedback

- Opportunities for collaborative problem solving

- Structured learning in increasing challenges

- Opportunity to mastery and level up

- Social connections

Gamification in the Classroom

Imagine entering a classroom with pupils who work independently or in groups and compete to be the best at answering questions from the teacher, who leads a lesson so engaging and motivating as to eliminate any form of boredom or repetitiveness. This may sound like science fiction. Yet it does not seem impossible, as long as we rethink the new concepts of knowledge transfer and create capable teaching experiences to include narrative and playful elements, as happens with the use of gamification. Although it is one of the most discussed topics in the field of training, the attempts to formulate a complete definition of gamification are far from reaching a conclusion. The expression gamification has become institutionalized and although not immune to criticism, it is widely used. But what are we talking about when we use the term *gamification* in reference to education?

According to Deterding[2], the term is currently used in reference to several related concepts, such as the growing diffusion and omnipresence of games and video games in everyday life, and the use of specific elements of the game to capture the attention of students in contexts that are traditionally far from entertainment. For example, training and learning. In general, the purpose is to involve users and encourage them to reach determined goals by following pre-established rules and possibly have fun.

Gamification has applications in many areas of daily life, such as those characterized by repetitive, boring, or aversive actions, which can include learning. As an example, Foursquare was a social network based on the geolocation of users in which there are points, prizes, rankings based on the frequency and ability of use of the system.

It is evident that, although the pervasiveness of playful and video game elements in modern times is a relatively recent and closely related phenomenon to the massive diffusion of digital technologies, the definition suggested by Deterding[2] is applicable to a much longer time span, in particular with reference to training. The game has always been used as a tool for didactic purposes, from the youngest age groups, and there are many cited examples of "educational" games that were able to develop skills and abilities such as concentration, memory, and manual skills.

---

[2] Deterding S., Paideia as Paidia: From Game-Based Learning to a Life Well-Played, 15 Giugno, 2012, Madison, Wisconsin, http://codingconduct.cc/Paideia-as-Paidia

Figure 7-2 shows the gamification elements present in training processes.

Training   Feedback   Progress track   Goal and Objective

Motivation   Team Build   Communication   Engaging storytelling

Figure 7-2. *Gamification elements in training processes*

Basically, by inserting one or more of the aforementioned elements in the training processes, you are more likely to involve and motivate students and encourage faster classroom learning. effective. The teacher can incorporate essential facts for didactic purposes in a narrative context and start the learning process by providing a challenge to the participants. This can start from an elementary level to progressively more difficult homework and finally to evaluate the expected learning outcomes.

It should not be forgotten that Generations Y and Z have different ways of perception and understanding reality, time, and space. They consequently have new learning needs that they are less reconciled with the traditional rules of frontal teaching.

They take the web for granted, they often use video games intensively and early in their lives, and they have an understanding of social media that's clearly different from their predecessors. The gap between the generations of so-called "boomers" born after WWII and students defined as "gamers" is getting bigger. Table 7-1 summarizes the major differences that emerge from a comparison of these generations.

Table 7-1. *Differences Between the Boomer Generation and the Gamer Generation*

Perception of	Boomer	Gamer
Knowledge	Structured (books, memory, standard operating procedures)	Unstructured (instant messaging blog, email)
Organizational structure	Hierarchical	Horizontal
Communication channels	Face to face phone	Informal (instant messaging blog, email)
Software application	Separate interface and information	Information and interface
Career Learning environment	Slow forward Classroom	Quick Online Advancement
Videogames	Distraction, entertainment, waste of time	Lifestyle
Information processing	Learning	Multitasking

The generation of the so-called gamers was born and formed in a context of the growing diffusion of technology and enormous information redundancy. They experience reality through rapid, interactive, and often non-linear processes and build their future on a highly global horizon, hence the inadequacy of traditional forms of learning.

The use of playful elements in the classroom does not replace textbooks and it does not mimic prizes, medals, and scores. It gives students an experience through which to develop knowledge, skills, and attitudes from a cognitive, relational, and behavioral point of view, all in a learning context characterized by a high level of active involvement. The advantages of using playful elements for learning purposes are multiple, as shown in Figure 7-3.

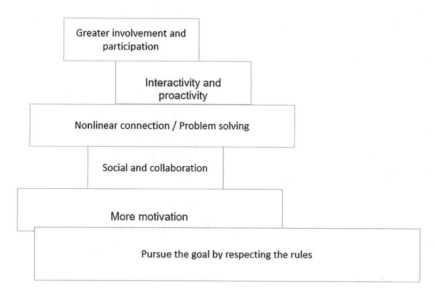

Figure 7-3. *Advantages of the use of playful elements in learning*

Games can be used for short demonstrations in one lesson or, in more complex cases, used as the main learning activity. Still, they can be part of a homework assignment.

Once the specific didactic objectives have been identified, the teacher can identify the game and the most congenial playful elements to offer to students, in order to improve their level of attention, involvement, and interactivity. This can add to the achievement of the original objectives pursued with innovative methods, the advantages in terms of pleasantness of experience, cohesion of the working group, and greater responsibility and autonomy of the participants.

Factors that Make Gamification in the Classroom Easier

Starting from the success of video games and online role-playing games, gamification has benefited from the use of the most advanced simulation technologies to promote learning in teaching and training. On the basis of what can be observed in modern gamified applications of a didactic nature, the following factors can facilitate gamification.

- **Realism.** The applications must be realistic, otherwise students can become disinterested or frustrated.

- **Challenge.** The pupil participating in the teaching experience must feel in competition with themselves and with the other students.

- **Personalization.** The ability to adapt the environment game allows players to operate in conditions of greater comfort and focus attention on operational details.

- **Acknowledgment of results.** Advancement from one level to another is very important in games, and to allow schoolchildren to make themselves known. Accounting for progress through incremental results is critical to keep interest alive.

- **Reputation.** Because students are motivated by recognition of the other classmates belonging to the same community, the solutions that exploit the mechanisms of the games and guarantee that the reputation of the pupils can always be improved by inserting a motivating augmentation mechanism.

In the presence of these conditions, gamification is finding increasing popularity as a self-guided training tool and it's replacing or supplementing other forms of training, such as tutorials, instructional videos, and classroom training.

The player works through the lesson in the form of a game, and actions or choices made are evaluated according to the didactic plan. Tips and guided assistance can be activated when the player makes a wrong choice, and the choices give life to scores and prizes. The player can work at their own pace and the interactive nature of this type of training can therefore increase the retention of the lesson content.

How Can Gamification Help with Learning?

Gamification in the school environment represents an evolutionary step in the way in which teachers and students will interact in the coming years. School, as it is conceived today, is not intended for the present generations and risks not channeling the potential of millions of young people in the best possible way.

Something is slowly changing, for example in the Anglo-Saxon world there are numerous institutes and teachers who have introduced gamified applications as an integral part of their teaching front, with numerous advantages. Through the use of these gamified applications, using smartphones or tablets, the student's brain is pushed to produce dopamine, which is a substance that carries information between the cells in the nervous system. Dopamine has several functions in the brain and plays a crucial role in directing attention and memory and encouraging the creation of connections between neurons. These *synapses* are the physical bases of learning.

Students appear to be active as they manipulate objects and they are in control of their actions, but above all, they are busy in empirical learning. This leads them to learn by doing and are immersed in scenarios and settings that are difficult to represent in reality. This stimulates cooperation and reflection. All this favors the long-term memorization of ideas, thanks to frequent references to the concepts in the application.

The teachers observed that gamification developed skills such as teamwork, communication, collaboration, and problem solving. Teachers who used gamified applications for educational purposes on a daily basis were able to obtain an increase in the level of participation of students in their own lessons.

All this helped to personalize the teaching experience and a collect information from schoolchildren. In fact, students appear to be at ease and more productive when tools closer to gaming are implemented at school, and due to rankings forms and competition in the gamification platform, they help keep motivation high. The main barrier to the adoption of these new teaching forms lies with the associated costs and the lack of basic technological infrastructures in the schools, such as smartphones, tablets, multimedia boards, and Wi-Fi. Figure 7-4 shows how gamification facilitates learning. There is also a difference between games-based learning and gamification-based learning and the next section will touch on this point.

Games-Based Learning vs Gamification

Often used interchangeably, the terms *gamification* and *game-based learning* are more and more frequently when it comes to didactic strategies aimed at making the learning processes delivered in e-learning mode more engaging.

While both are innovative methods of training students, they should not be used interchangeably.

We therefore try to understand how they can be applied to the logic, design, structure, and dynamics of video games. By definition, gamification is a strategy aimed at applying mechanics, dynamics, and typical elements of the game in contexts that are not purely playful to support specific behaviors.

In e-learning, the use of these mechanisms is aimed at motivating and involving learners, making it an active part of their learning process. It is no coincidence that a large part of e-learning experiences are embracing gamification.

Using gamification makes sense when you have to:

1. Solicit certain responses or behaviors from students.

2. Increase visibility and perception of the importance of certain actions otherwise considered minor.

3. Promote competition and engage and involve students.

4. Help students track their progress and efforts.

Game-based learning is achieved through the use of video games, which can sometimes be born as entertainment tools, but which are then reused, with or without modifications, to achieve an educational goal. Game-based learning does not necessarily involve playing video games. This practice can also consist of using logic, design principles, the architecture of the video game, its mechanics, and its own dynamics.

When playing a video game or reconfiguring the learning process according to the architecture of the video game, students are forced to learn the rules of the game, address the understanding of complex systems, adopt various types of tactics, manage the complexity produced by the interaction of multiple systemic elements and variables, and know how to constantly adapt their own behavior to the constant change of the context of the world in which they play.

Using game-based learning makes sense when you need to:

1. Reconfigure the disciplinary contents.

2. Promote critical and strategic thinking.

3. Involve students who do not engage in any other way.

4. Help pupils in need and support talented pupils.

Gamification and game-based learning both promote practice, constant exercise, commitment, collaboration, learning by trial and error, constancy, strategic thinking, and many other cognitive and metacognitive abilities. Both terms offer interesting opportunities to make the e-learning experience more engaging.

The trick lies in choosing the right approach and taking into consideration the domain to be treated, the results to be obtained, and above all the students and their formative needs.

Solutions for an Educational Game

The development of didactic applications is a multimedia production that requires much higher design skills than digital production for the web. For the realization of a multimedia educational game, there are various tools. Some do not require programming skills, while others do, including these noted here:

- **CryEngine and Godot** are two outstanding game engines that can be utilized for game production.

- **Machinations** are "game feedback diagrams," i.e., interactive flow diagrams for games. These are free tools that can be used simply online. A conceptual framework is a diagrammatic tool that focuses on structural features of game mechanics. They naturally shape the side management of the game when resource management is important. This isn't useful in fictional or dynamic games. It does not require knowledge of programming languages.

- **GameMaker Studio** is a product created to allow creation of 2D games without having to write code. The games are composed through dragging and dropping components. It does not require knowledge of programming.

- **HTML5 prototypes** are simple and easily shareable ways to create games through the use of JavaScript in the browser. Developing HTML5 prototypes is particularly straightforward for narrative modeling and testing. It requires basic HTML5 and JavaScript proficiency.

- **Paper prototyping** is one of the techniques used to approach a game's design. Using cards, dice, and board game components, you can create simulations for certain families of games. However, most popular games have an algorithmic aspect, for example artificial intelligence, and the response rate of the feedback is constitutive of the gaming experience. These aspects cannot be reproduced on paper. This highlights how much the design of educational games requires specific skills that are quite different than traditional game design.

- **Unity Game Engine** is a very popular tool, thanks to its power, its multi-platform support, from smartphones to consoles, and its developer community. It provides numerous ready-to-use components.

- **Unreal Engine** is one of the most powerful frameworks for creating games and until recently it had very high initial costs so it was not used except in the context of large productions. But Unreal has reduced costs and commissions, and has become a viable solution. You do need a development team with considerable technical experience and a game involving 3D environments.

- **HTML5 and PhoneGap solutions** are various solutions that use browsers to create games and then a form of packaging to allow the solution to be usable as an application independent from the browser. PhoneGap from Adobe is one such solution. The power of these solutions lies in the typographic support (standard in HTML5), the simplicity of programming, and the wide compatibility of platforms, thus allowing for a timely publication relatively quickly.

This last solution was used for the next sections of this chapter and is explained in detail in the following sections.

Designing a Gamified Application

This section discusses educational games dedicated to the learning of children and focuses on the topic of mathematics. It also discusses the design choices for this project, which is a mobile application designed to help students learn mathematics thanks to a series of challenges and targeted exercises. The technologies used to create mobile applications are then illustrated, specifically the techniques of development and programming languages.

Math Games for Kids

This mobile application helps students learn mathematical operations. In trying to define a possible game mechanic, it references the universe of existing games and teaching methods. This theme has tried to create fun games and use the characteristics of the video game to create innovative learning methods. Educational games cannot be low-quality games, because the target is used to high-quality games.

You cannot just present boring and repetitive game mechanics, but it is necessary to work a lot on gameplay and use elements you notice that lead the student to raise their expectations. One point that had to be kept in mind during the design of the educational game is the competence of the student. When they acquire a skill in a game, that skill should be used later in various forms.

Another aspect is the integration between classroom and leisure time activities and possible integration with a community that goes beyond the school group. As mentioned, attempts to create an application that teaches something as a primary goal have often proved unsuccessful. In order to avoid the repetition of these errors, this mathematics app was designed with the goal to entertain the users, not to instruct them.

Within it, each element has been designed to be part of a game system more than a learning one. To do this, there are the four player profiles—one for each type of user for which the application was designed. It is important to consider that it is precisely these players who must be involved in the application, but we must not make the mistake of considering them pupils to teach.

Learning must be stimulated and induced, but never forced and always voluntary, just as fun is. Each of the four categories has its strengths and issues, and all the previous suggestions on how to be implementing certain mechanisms take them into account in equal measure.

The app was designed to offer a fun and educational experience regardless of personality, but taking into account the characteristics of all types of players and the interactions that each has with the others.

For example, the medals are clearly associated with the profile of the Achievers, but the context of the team competition aims at the synergistic involvement of Killers and Socializers, without excluding or isolating Explorers and Achievers. Among the various elements that attract players are goals and medals.

The application provides a section dedicated to the summary of medals, obtained and not, where the players can see the successes achieved and check the future goals to aim for. These medals are unlocked based on different parameters. The time and effort required to obtain them must respect a curve of growth such that the user is not discouraged but also not awarded too easily. This method is common practice in user design, as it helps to focus attention on the needs, objectives, desires, and limitations of the various types of users. Table 7-2 was used as a basis for implementing this project, which creates an application designed to help students be better prepared in mathematics.

Table 7-2. *Basic Gamification Checklist for the Mathematics Project*

	PLAYERS		FRAMEWORK	
ACTIVITY	**1. Motivation**	**2. Relevant choices**	**3. Structure**	**3. Potential conflicts**
Helping students to be better prepared in mathematics through an app.	A) Increase the amount of students who manage to pass an assignment or exam. B) Promote and improve social interaction between classes and classes and study.	Students who are better at better subject can positively influence students . The latter receive input from their peers who have been in the same situation as themselves.	The answers are given through the approval of the students for the students. This can include points, titles, badges, achievements or a combination of all.	Nothing however this should not be seen as a substitute for ordinary lessons or teachings, but rather as a supplement.

Gamified Applications Dedicated to Training

One of the sectors in which gamification opens more interesting scenarios is certainly that of training, in all its forms, from school education to self-study. Gamification, in fact, adds motivational elements to a system of training to increase student involvement.

The fact that gamification in training shows enormous potential is not surprising, considering the close relationship between gaming and learning. In fact, the game represents one of the ancestral methods that we have always worked to learn, because it is the most natural tool with which our brain learns. Many outdated and ineffective training models still rely on one tell-test logic, in which the student is seen only as a passive receptor of notions.

Today training is no longer limited to transmitting knowledge, but also concerns the ability to involve students in stimulating their interests and grabbing their attention. Play as discussed at beginning of this chapter is a cognitive tool that's mainly self-directed, in which the subject is the active protagonist. It's precisely this feature that maximizes the effectiveness of learning. Some significant didactic experiences are analyzed next and they use elements of successful gamification, as shown in the Figure 7-4.

ClassDojo

ClassDojo[3] is an application that helps teachers manage their class by facilitating the immediacy and strength of feedback, stimulating continuous improvement of pupils, and ultimately creating a more interactive and fruitful learning environment.

ClassDojo allows teachers to help their pupils reflect on their progress and to encourage certain behaviors through virtual recognition and timely feedback. (It should be borne in mind that the brain is made up of two hemispheres. The right hemisphere is the most irrational, instinctive, and impulsive part through which individuality and a creative vision are expressed. The left hemisphere is the most reflective part and it evaluates all the data in our possession in a rational, analytical way, orienting one's choices in the best possible way.)

ClassDojo is also a tool for engaging parents and communicating with them in an immediate way through reports and statistics that can be printed or sent by email. But the advantages are above all for students, as each player in the system:

---

[3] ClassDojo App Android, 2013, https://play.google.com/store/apps/details?id=com.classdojo.android&hl=it.

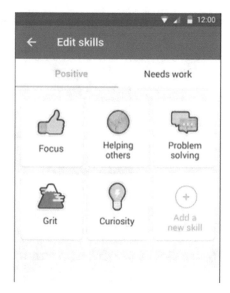

Figure 7-4. *Use of Gamification strategies with feedback and targeted learning*

- Corresponds to an avatar that represents the player (the avatar constitutes a virtual projection of self and therefore refers to the core drive of possession).

- Is able to monitor the evolution of their skills in real time (in this case, we are talking about levels and rankings so the reference is to core drive of possession).

- Can see the achieved results and be rewarded for virtuous behavior (rewards and positive feedback are shared with the rest of the class, therefore, virtuous behaviors are triggered which can be traced back to the core drive of relationality). How the brain and motivation are correlated is shown in Figure 7-5.

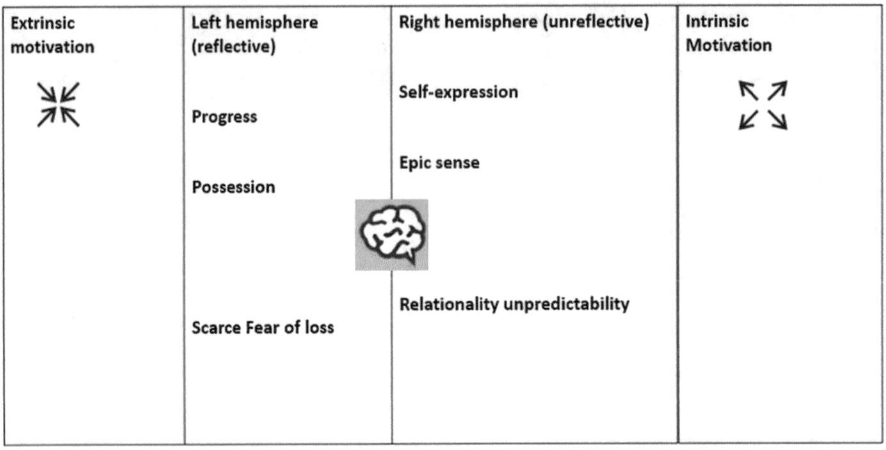

Extrinsic motivation	Left hemisphere (reflective)	Right hemisphere (unreflective)	Intrinsic Motivation
⇲⇱⇲⇱	Progress	Self-expression	⇱⇲⇱⇲
	Possession	Epic sense	
		Relationality unpredictability	
	Scarce Fear of loss		

Figure 7-5. *Core drives, areas of the brain, and motivations*

Specifically, progress, possession, scarcity, and fear of loss are rational levers because they concern both logic and calculation and they represent extrinsic motivations. While self-expression, epic sense, relationality, and unpredictability, on the other hand, concern the irrational sphere and represent intrinsic motivations. These levers have been extensively analyzed and exploited by game designers and are the basis of the design of every gamified application.

Methodology for Creating Gamified Applications

The development of wireless technologies and the enormous diffusion of more powerful devices has pushed many institutions in the direction of teaching via mobile platforms. Many educational institutions are using gamified applications to stay close to their students.

A section later in this chapter will illustrate, by means of a practical case, how it is possible create a web app in the field of mathematics by adopting elements of gamification. There are two basic approaches to making the user of a mobile device interact with an application. The first is represented by the interaction with a web page, by browsing a network, i.e., the whole pages available on the world wide web, or page navigation offline.

The other approach is the creation of a targeted and specific application for a certain type of smartphone, tablet, or operating system. In the two cases described previously, we speak of web applications (web apps) and native applications. The following sections discuss the main differences and explain how the two approaches are related to the topic of gamified applications.

Web Application

A web application (web app) is an application that's accessible via the web through a network, such as an intranet or the Internet. This application model has become quite popular, in consideration of the possibility for a generic client to access application functions, using web browsers as normal terminals.

In fact, the opportunity to upgrade and evolve at a reduced cost application, without being forced to distribute numerous updates to its users through physical media, has made this solution the optimal method to pursue. In the case of a smartphone or tablet, it is possible to log in via a data or wireless connection.

In general, we speak of a web application when the function performed by the page is more than just a consultation. Its content is in general dynamic and interactive. What can be called a web app includes software such as webmail, e-commerce sites, web forums, blogs, and online games. The "window" that allows the user to interact with these applications is the browser. Typically, this type of software is built using programming languages that leave the computation and management of the behavior of the page to the server.

The code of the page in this case is compiled on the server side, the web page is provided by the browser without the programming code. This makes the management of the page safe, as the user will not know how the data is handled. The alternative to creating a web application is to rely on HTML5, CCS3, and JavaScript code.

This code will be inside the page, and it will be up to the web browser to interpret and manage it. The advantages of web app development include the following points:

- Development costs represent a small part of the project, and you can use plug-ins with jQuery Mobile to facilitate the implementation work.

- They are quick to develop as they do not require relevant technical skills. In fact, the app is created with the use of HTML, CSS, and JavaScript.

- Web applications can run on any device that has a web browser.

- Users will use the same version.

- Bugs can be fixed in real time.

The disadvantages in developing web applications are the following:

- Not all hardware features of the phone can be accessed.

- It can be difficult to achieve sophisticated effects in the user interface.

This chapter takes the web app from the web to a mobile environment, which is the PhoneGap framework. It represents a sandbox that contains the web pages and allows you to make the leap toward almost all the mobile platforms present on the market. The following sections explain how and through which standards the PhoneGap framework, used for the design of the web, operates. See Figure 7-6.

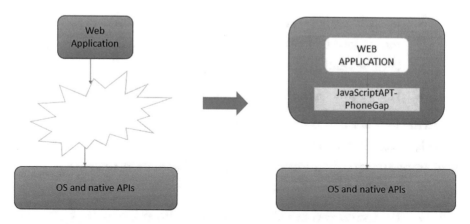

Figure 7-6. *PhoneGap encloses the web application and accesses the OS API*

Native Application

A native mobile application is created specifically for one or more platforms and normally contains a large amount of data. This involves the use of the appropriate programming language, the installation of an application development package, also called an SDK (Software Development Kit), and platform development related to the target system. For some proprietary platforms, it is also necessary to use suitable hardware to compile the applications.

The advantages of the native approach include:

- An increase in performance, because it speeds up and simplifies the use of data, which partly resides on the mobile device.

- Ability to access all the hardware features of the device.

- Does not depend on access to the network.

257

- Is easily available, because it's found within the manufacturer's virtual application stores and is certified and guaranteed by it.

- Higher precision in the creation of the user interface.

In the face of a commitment of design and coding, you may have to design every detail of the application manually in order to make its appearance unique. In addition to the points listed here, the native approach has the following disadvantages:

- It must be developed on a specific platform.

- Bug fixes cannot be released in a timely manner.

- The development cycle is slow, and the testing cycle is constrained by the limitations of the store they belong to.

Native App vs Web App

It is difficult to say with certainty which approach is best to follow. In fact, as previously described, both approaches have advantages and disadvantages.

According to Thomas Husson of Forrester Research[4], native and web applications coexist at the moment and will continue to do so in the future, by virtue of reciprocal evolutions. Browsers will evolve rapidly and will be increasingly integrated with the hardware components of smartphones.

Even markup languages are evolving. The evolution of the mobile web will also push a large improvement in native applications, which will also be able to go deep even in areas so far little explored, such as education.

---

[4] Husson T., Mobile App Or Mobile Web? For It, It's A Choice, Not A Battle, 2013, https://www.forrester.com/Mobile+App+Or+Mobile+Web+For+IT+Its+A+Choice +Not +A+Battle/fulltext/-/E-res107481#AST957523

The choice between native applications and web applications depends on many factors, especially on the users you want to reach. The dividing line between a web application and a native application becomes more and more subtle. Several third-party projects, among which the best known is PhoneGap, are actively developing some solutions that allow web developers to transform a web app into a native application for mobile platforms.

This represents the perfect blend, and as previously described, is the solution adopted for this app. All these technologies are evolving, so more and more will be needed in order to consider a multi-platform approach across different devices such as smartphones, tablets, PCs, and even smart TVs.

The PhoneGap Framework

When it comes to games on the mobile platform, creating mobile apps is always a challenge. We presently have three separate mobile platforms (Android, iOS, and Windows Phone), each with its own development framework and a variety of mobile development frameworks that help with code sharing and development. This section discusses a recent study for determining the optimal framework for designing mobile applications. Hybrid apps are the best option for quickly developing a mobile app that is favorably received by users.

We utilize the framework to compare Adobe PhoneGap to native development on the Android and the Windows Phone. Many studies show that, while the cross-platform approach is simple to use, the app's design and usability were at best subpar.

PhoneGap is an open-source development tool and was originally created by the Canadian company Nitobi, as well as by a large community of developers, including some from IBM, RIM, and Microsoft.

It consists of a set of static libraries that allow you to quickly and effectively develop applications for different mobile device families. The fundamental idea of this project is to try to achieve the slogan, "Write once, port everywhere."

PhoneGap aims to focus developers' efforts on the application rather than wasting time adapting it to each platform. Essentially its goal is very simple: to provide developers lacking specific knowledge regarding the different platforms one tool that allows them to write cross-platform applications in the world as simply and quickly as possible. To do this, an application created with PhoneGap requires knowledge of HTML5, CSS3, and JavaScript. Porting to the various platforms is done by installing the development environments and compiling the web app. The requirements are then to install the SDKs, when required by the platform, and the tools that allow the applications to be compiled (see Figure 7-7).

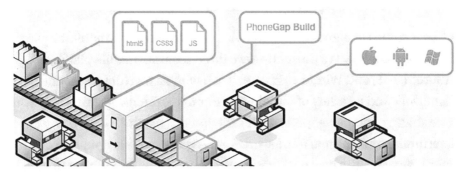

Figure 7-7. *Porting processes to different mobile platforms*

PhoneGap is nothing more than a wrapper, a container that allows developers to embed their web applications within native applications to different platforms.

Why PhoneGap?

Choosing a good cross-platform framework for developing mobile applications is of fundamental importance. In the phases that characterize the realization of an application—in general analysis, design, implementation, and testing—it is convenient to use tools that facilitate the various phases. Furthermore, all this translates to a considerable saving of resources and time. A quality framework is also recognized by the reputation of the software house that produces it.

In the case of PhoneGap, we are talking about Adobe Systems, a company that has been in business for decades and has always built quality products. It should also be remembered that a multi-platform framework such as PhoneGap allows access to the native APIs of the specific mobile environment, and not all existing frameworks support all features. Another feature to note concerns the release times of the new versions of a given framework.

Relatively frequent releases give developers the opportunity to understand that the framework in question is followed and used by many and therefore reaches advanced stages of development, which means they allow the implementation of more and more complete functionalities. The possibility of expanding the features of one framework is another point in favor, since the most important software projects are always accompanied by large communities of enthusiasts.

These enthusiasts often develop plug-ins third parties and create extensive documentation accompanying these extensions. Finally, we must always think about the goal of the mobile application.

There are open-source and commercial projects that require different attention for the subsequent deployment phase. As for commercial projects, whose goal is monetization, the use of suitable licenses is fundamental. If you do not want to invest in development tools that in turn adopt commercial licenses, it is necessary to use professional tools that are based on MIT and open-source licenses.

The choice of using PhoneGap for porting an application to the Android environment was dictated by all the features discussed here. Comparing the PhoneGap framework to other competitors led to the choice of PhoneGap, as it responded to needs of this mathematics application.

With PhoneGap, developers can devote themselves to the development of the web application without thinking about the hindrances or impediments of the various platforms.

Clearly the possibilities are limited to those of a web application. Some key aspects to evaluate in deciding whether to exploit the PhoneGap framework for your project are the following:

- Despite the fact that all platforms are aligning with standards of HTML5, some allow other functionality beyond that offered by PhoneGap. It is necessary to evaluate your needs and to keep aware of the possibility of using these features.

- During the development phase, drafting HTML pages needs some attention in the development of the JavaScript part. Each platform has its own native browser and handles that code differently.

- Regardless of the operating system of the target platform, a rigorous testing phase is required to verify its operation.

- As future prospects, it is desirable that each platform improves in the native browser. By improving the rendering of web pages, you improve the applications created in PhoneGap.

- If you have a working web application, maybe already developed using HTML5, porting it to mobile platforms is very easy.

To date, the platforms covered by PhoneGap are currently almost the entire market, and it is possible to find an updated list of many of them on the PhoneGap website.[5]

PhoneGap's Architecture

The PhoneGap architecture is divided into four software levels—the operating system level, the PhoneGap native level, the PhoneGap JavaScript level, and the application layer.

The operating system level represents the lowest level of the framework PhoneGap. It is the part that comes closest to the structure of the operating system on which the application is run. When developing a native application, you can access this level directly using the tools made available by the manufacturer of the operating system (SDK), thus exploiting the native APIs provided by the environment.

The native layer of PhoneGap, also called the PhoneGap Bridge layer, allows the browser, in particular the WebView, to access the functionalities that are native to the device. Using this level, PhoneGap developers have created a first part of the "bridge" that links the JavaScript code to the native code of each environment.

In addition, the "PhoneGap bridge layer" contains another software component, called "Webkit View," which allows you to run applications created by developers (see Figure 7-8). The JavaScript layer of PhoneGap represents the second part of the "bridge," which is created in the PhoneGap Bridge Layer. It contains the second part of the code that allows you to link JavaScript scripts to the native environment of the device.

---

[5] PhoneGap Apps, Apps Created with PhoneGap, 2015, http://phonegap.com/app/

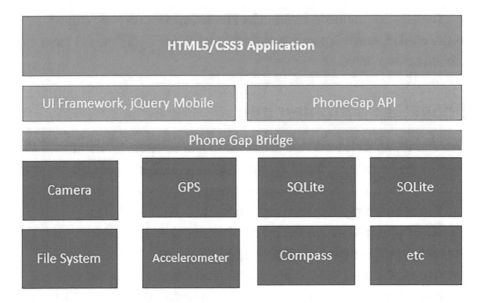

Figure 7-8. *Architecture for PhoneGap*

This level also contains the APIs defined by the PhoneGap framework, which act as wrappers to access the real APIs of each mobile platform. This part of the architecture can be considered the "heart" of PhoneGap, as it contains the interfaces for accessing the native features of the operating system, thus allowing access through appropriate scripts to the functions described previously.

To avoid frequent cases of overhead, the PhoneGap functions natively implemented in the WebView are redirected through this level to the native APIs, which can be accessed through the underlying levels. Finally, the application layer represents the highest and most abstract layer of PhoneGap. It contains the application created by the developer in HTML5, CSS3, and JavaScript.

The only layers of the PhoneGap architecture accessible to the developer are the application layer and the interface of the JavaScript layer. All other levels are not visible to a PhoneGap programmer, due to the encapsulation principle. The application can hide information by encapsulating it in a construct with an interface, allowing information hiding.

Encapsulation reduces the cost to be paid to correct errors in the phase development of an application. This is achieved by structuring the entire project, and the modules that make it up, so that an erroneous decision taken in the implementation of a single module is not reflected on the entire project and can be corrected by modifying only that module. In the initial PhoneGap architecture, the JavaScript and native layers were united into a single layer. With the introduction of plug-ins, it was necessary to separate these layers.

They have been redesigned and made into components, separated by their functionality of access to the native API. The ability to include third-party plug-ins expands the potential of PhoneGap. The use of such plug-ins is flexible thanks to the ability to link them, both natively and through JavaScript. This is necessary because plug-ins always consist of a native part that executes the code and a JavaScript part that provides the interfaces between the application and the native code that runs.

The plug-ins, therefore, are not cross-platform and the two parts must be developed for each mobile platform. The model of programming on which PhoneGap is based involves the use of techniques used in web applications and in particular is divided into design of two main components: the graphic interface and the logic of the application. The graphic interface is implemented using HTML and CSS, in the same way a web application is created. However, there are some precautions that must be adopted in order to avoid problems related to interface rendering.

Mobile devices, in addition to being characterized by a wide range of video resolutions, can also be used in landscape and portrait mode. This implies the use of specific techniques for the creation of mobile web apps, such as media queries.

The application logic is implemented using JavaScript, with which you have full access to the computational capability of the device. Furthermore, thanks to the PhoneGap architecture, it is possible to access objects made available by the API, with which you can manipulate some hardware functionality of the system on which the application is run. JavaScript logic, like web applications, follows the mechanism of event capture.

The programming model provides event management using traditional JavaScript event handlers through PhoneGap events. With the event handlers provided by JavaScript, you can capture all the events that occur in the Document Object Model. The PhoneGap events, on the other hand, allow you to differentiate an application web from a multi-platform mobile application, since in this case it will be possible to capture events closely related to the device.

The three main technologies used to build web applications are HTML5, CCS3, and JavaScript. These three languages help create the structure of the web page (HTML), personalize its appearance (CSS), and make it dynamic and interactive (JavaScript code). See Figure 7-9.

Figure 7-9. *Technologies used to build web applications*

In addition to these and for the realization of this gamified mathematics application, I also used the jQuery Mobile framework, PHP, AJAX, and JSON. All these technologies will be illustrated.

Now let's discuss common Python frameworks for developing GUIs. We have gathered some of the most popular Python GUI frameworks in our list and they are listed next. They can be used for HCI based game development.

Anaconda Python and the PyQT5 GUI Framework

In order to take an HCI approach, Anaconda Python and the PyQT5 GUI framework are used for application development. In this section, you learn about the Anaconda Python distribution framework, including how to interface with the Python interpreter, how to utilize the conda package management, and how to install the PyQT5 GUI framework.

Anaconda Installation

Anaconda is a Python distribution that includes over 400 of the most widely used Python programs for science, mathematics, technology, and data analysis. We'll utilize it because of some of its package characteristics, even if it's aimed at the academic programming community. Conda, the package manager included with Anaconda, allows you to install and upgrade packages. Anaconda provides tools for creating virtual Python setups with the precise packages (and package versions) that you require. Anaconda's settings may be used to keep a working environment separate from the rest of the world.

We've previously double-checked that the PyQT5 packages are functional (at least for Windows and Linux). Miniconda, a smaller variant of Anaconda, will be used.

Linux

There is a shell script installer for Linux systems. Download and execute it with the following command:

```
bash Miniconda3-latest-Linux-x86_64.sh
```

Note   You do not need to run this with `sudo`.

Windows

Windows only has the graphical installer. Download and execute it.

PyQT5 Installation

Test driving with Conda. Conda is the name of the Anaconda package management system. It neatly encapsulates all package installation and setup operations. It also takes care of your virtual Python environments. Like `pip`, it's easy to install and it works nicely with other Python package management systems. It simply makes life better.

Follow this Conda lesson for more information:

`http://conda.pydata.org/docs/test-drive.html`

Linux

This works on Linux (Ubuntu 16) and should work on macOS:

```
conda create -n pyqt5 ipython pyqt
conda activate pyqt5
```

Windows

Launch the Miniconda installer. When it finishes, search for the Anaconda prompt and run it. Then, this should work:

```
conda create -n pyqt5 ipython pyqt
conda activate pyqt5
```

PyQt5 Example

Run this script in an IPython shell. Instantiate one of each of the defined classes and observe the printed messages. You can find this code using the following link:

https://github.com/JosephThachilGeorge/pyqt5_lab

Inheritance

```
class A:                        # Base class
    def __init__(self):         # With constructor
        print('initializing A.')

    def m1(self):
        print('A.m1()')

class B(A):                 # Inherit from A.
    def m1(self):           # Override m1.
        print(' B.m1()')

class C(A):                     # Inherit from A
    def __init__(self):         # Override constructor.
        print('initializing C.')

class D(A):                     # Make sure to call super
constructor.
```

```python
def __init__(self):
    A.__init__(self)
    print('initializing D.')
```

Skeleton

```python
# Import stuff
import sys
from PyQt5.QtWidgets import QApplication, QLabel, QMainWindow

# Use a __main__ guard, you never know.
if __name__ == '__main__':
    # Create our application -- MUST be done first.
    app = QApplication(sys.argv)

    # Create a main window with a single QLabel.
    window = QMainWindow()
    label = QLabel('Hello PyQT5!')
    window.setCentralWidget(label)

    # Show the main window and call main loop.
    window.show()
    app.exec_()
```

Buttons

```python
# Import stuff
import sys
from PyQt5.QtWidgets import QApplication, QPushButton,
QMainWindow

# Use a __main__ guard, you never know.
if __name__ == '__main__':
    # Create our application -- MUST be done first.
    app = QApplication(sys.argv)
```

```
# Create a main window with a single QLabel.
window = QMainWindow()
button = QPushButton('Hello PyQT5!')
window.setCentralWidget(button)

# Show the main window and call main loop.
window.show()
app.exec_()
```

Layout

```
# Import stuff
import sys
from PyQt5.QtWidgets import QApplication, QPushButton,
QMainWindow, QLabel
from PyQt5.QtWidgets import QBoxLayout, QWidget

if __name__ == '__main__':
    app = QApplication(sys.argv)
    app.setStyleSheet('QPushButton { font-size: 48pt; }')

    # Create a main window, a placeholder widget, and a layout.
    window = QMainWindow()
    widget = QWidget()
    layout = QBoxLayout(QBoxLayout.TopToBottom)

    # Set the layout for our widget to the vbox.
    widget.setLayout(layout)
    window.setCentralWidget(widget)

    # Add some buttons.
    buttons = [QPushButton('Button {}'.format(i)) for i in
    range(5)]
    for b in buttons:
        layout.addWidget(b)
```

```
window.show()
app.exec_()
```

Event

```
import sys
from PyQt5.QtWidgets import QApplication, QPushButton,
QMainWindow
from PyQt5.QtWidgets import QBoxLayout, QWidget

# This is the *slot* we will connect to button presses.
def clicky():
    print('Clicky clicky!')

if __name__ == '__main__':
    app = QApplication(sys.argv)
    app.setStyleSheet('QPushButton { font-size: 48pt; }')
    window = QMainWindow()
    widget = QWidget()
    layout = QBoxLayout(QBoxLayout.TopToBottom)
    widget.setLayout(layout)
    window.setCentralWidget(widget)

    # Add some buttons.
    buttons = [QPushButton('Button {}'.format(i)) for i in
    range(5)]
    for b in buttons:
        b.clicked.connect(clicky)  # Connect the clicked signal
        to clicky()
        layout.addWidget(b)

    # Show the main window and call main loop.
    window.show()
    app.exec_()
```

PyQT Events

This section shows you how to create a non-trivial graphical application. You can achieve this by utilizing some of the PyQT5 framework's powerful event processing features. We'll look at how observable objects may be used to decentralize application functionality and make components less aware of one another.

You can find the code at the following link :

https://github.com/JosephThachilGeorge/pyqt_events_lab.

```
#
# In this exercise you will work with QTimers and this simple
# CounterButton implementation.
#
# 1. Implement a simple QApplication that uses the
     CounterButton
#    class. Make a layout that contains a few
     CounterButtons (say,5)
#    and displays them.
#
# 2. Now, set up a QTimer that, once every two seconds,
     *subtracts* 1
#    from the click count of the CounterButton. Observe the
     behavior
#    of your application.
#
```

Timers

```
import sys
from PyQt5.QtWidgets import QPushButton, QApplication

class CounterButton(QPushButton):
```

```
    '''Simple button widget that counts number of times
    clicked.'''
    def __init__(self, initval=0, **kwargs):
        super().__init__(**kwargs)
        self._counter = initval
        self.setText('Clicks: {}'.format(self._counter))

    def mouseReleaseEvent(self, event):
        self._counter = self._counter + 1
        self.setText('Clicks: {}'.format(self._counter))
        super().mouseReleaseEvent(event)
```

Runners

```
#
# The exercises are based on this below running example.
#
# 1. Take some time to make sure you understand *everything*
#    about #how this application works. It is our first non-
#    trivial example of #a
#PyQT5 Application, and your understanding of it will be
essential     #for the rest of the laboratory.
#
# 2. Create a new directory called 'RunningExample'. Copy
#    this file
#    into this new folder and call it 'main.py'. Working in
#    this new
#    directory, we will refactor this running example into
#    a better
#    designed implementation.
#
#
# Part I: Improving CounterButton
```

```
# --------------------------------
#
# 3. In the RunningExample directory, copy the
      'CounterButton' class
#     implementation into a file called 'counterbutton.py'.
      Change the
#     implementation to use as Observabel for the
      internal counter
#     instead of a bare field (like we saw in the lesson
      yesterday).
#
# 4. Change the 'main.py' file to use the new
      CounterButton class
#     implementation in 'counterbutton.py'.
#
# 5. Implement a simple test program *inside* the
      'counterbutton.py'
#     file that, when the file is *run* as a script, builds
      a simple
#     application with a stack of 5 CounterButtons. *HINT*:
      recall how
#     the __name__ guard is used to implement such
      functionality.
#
#
# Part II: Improving the ConfigPane implementation
# -----------------------------------------------
#
# 6. As before, copy the ConfigPane class implementation
      into a new
```

```
#      file called 'configpane.py'. Now change the
       implementation of
#      ConfigPane to use an *Observable* Python dict that
       maps *names*
#      of configuration parameters to their values (call this new
#      Observable 'configvals'). *NOTE*: you will have to
       change the
#      implementation of the 'get_param()' method to use this new
#      object. You might also think about implementing a
       set_param()
#      method... *hint* *hint*.
#
# 7. Add a callback 'on_configure' in the new ConfigPane
#      implementation that listens for clicks of the
       configure button
#      widget. In this callback, implement the logic to copy
       the text
#      values from the TextInput widgets into the configvals
#      Observable.
#
# 8. Finally, back in the main Application Class, bind a new
       callback
#      (call it on_configvals) to changes in 'configvals' in the
#      ConfigPane. In this callback, implement the logic to
       delete and
#      re-build the ButtonPane with the new configuration
       parameters.
#
#

import sys
```

```python
from PyQt5.QtWidgets import QPushButton, QApplication,
QMainWindow, QWidget, QGridLayout, QLineEdit, QLabel,
QTabWidget

class CounterButton(QPushButton):
    '''Simple button widget that counts number of times
    clicked.'''
    def __init__(self, initval=0, **kwargs):
        super().__init__(**kwargs)
        self._counter = initval
        self.setText('Clicks: {}'.format(self._counter))

    def mouseReleaseEvent(self, event):
        self._counter = self._counter + 1
        self.setText('Clicks: {}'.format(self._counter))
        super().mouseReleaseEvent(event)

class ConfigPane(QGridLayout):
    '''Panel of configuration options. Buggy and not very
    featureful.'''
    def __init__(self, params, on_configure, **kwargs):
        '''The constructor takes a list of integer params of
        the form (NAME, DEFAULT).'''
        super().__init__(**kwargs)
        self._textinputs = {}

        # Iterate over all config parameters.
        for (i, (p, d)) in enumerate(params):
            # Make the label and add it.
            label = QLabel(text=p)
            self.addWidget(label, i, 0)

            # Save the textinput in a local dict so we can
            # recover it by parameter *name*.
```

```
            self._textinputs[p] = QLineEdit(text=str(d))
            self.addWidget(self._textinputs[p], i, 1)

        # Add the reconfigure button, bind click to *user-
        provided*
        # on_configure callback. Messy.
        self._configbutton = QPushButton(text='Reconfigure')
        self._configbutton.clicked.connect(on_configure)
        self.addWidget(self._configbutton, len(params),
        0, 1, 2)

    # This is a simple interface to let us get parameters
    by *name*
    # from outside this class.
    def get_param(self, p):
        '''Return the configuration parameter from the
        textinput with label p.'''
        return int(self._textinputs[p].text())

# Class to hold a grid of CounterButtons.
class ButtonPane(QGridLayout):
    '''Widget that contains a number of CounterButtons arranged
    in a GridLayout.'''
    def __init__(self, num_buttons, cols=1, initval=0,
    **kwargs):
        super().__init__(**kwargs)

        # Logic to create a grid of CounterButtons in cols
        columns.
        for i in range(num_buttons):
            self.addWidget(CounterButton(initval=initval), i //
            cols, i % cols)

# The main application.
```

```
class TestApp(QApplication):
    '''The main application. The on_configure() method is called
    when the 'Reconfigure' button pressed on config pane.'''
    def __init__(self, args):
        # Root is a QTabWidget, first tab is ConfigPane, second
        a ButtonPane.
        super().__init__(args)
        self._root = QTabWidget()
        self._config = QWidget()
        self._buttons = QWidget()
        self._config.setLayout(ConfigPane(params=[('Columns',
        2), ('Buttons', 10)], on_configure=self.on_configure))
        self._buttons.setLayout(ButtonPane(num_buttons=10,
        cols=2))
        self._root.addTab(self._config, 'Configuration')
        self._root.addTab(self._buttons, 'Buttons')
        self._root.setFixedSize(640, 480)
        self._root.show()
        self.exec_()

    # This is the callback we pass into the constructor of
    ConfigPane
    # so that it can call us back with the Reonfigure button is
    # pressed. Super messy.
    def on_configure(self):
        '''Callback for re-configure request on config pane.'''
        cols = self._config.layout().get_param('Columns')
        buttons = self._config.layout().get_param('Buttons')
        self._root.removeTab(1)
        self._buttons = QWidget()
        self._buttons.setLayout(ButtonPane(num_buttons=buttons,
        cols=cols))
```

```
        self._root.addTab(self._buttons, 'Buttons')

# Instantiate and run the application.
app = TestApp(sys.argv)
```

These examples demonstrate how to utilize PyQt5 in gamification applications (GUI apps). PyQt5 is one of the most popular Python programming modules for creating graphical user interfaces, and this is owing to its ease of use, as you will discover. The PyQt5 architect, which makes it much easier to construct sophisticated GUI programs in a short amount of time, is another wonderful feature that motivates developers to choose PyQt5. To create a form, you simply drag and drop your components.

There are four main benefits to gamifying your mobile phone app:

1. **Incorporate your gamification app design:** Components will boost the longevity of your app, resulting in organic installations. This provides a better user experience and will inspire your users to recommend your software to their friends, resulting in organic installations. A fitness software with gamified aspects, for example, allows users to post their accomplishments on social media. This user-generated material is a clever way to raise brand recognition while also allowing users to share their accomplishments with friends and relatives.

2. **Motivate users and help retain them:** Gamification in mobile applications encourages users to stay engaged for longer periods of time. This can have a significant influence on your loyalty and attrition rates.

3. **Unleash consumer ingenuity:** You may unlock your users' ingenuity by gamifying features in your smartphone app, resulting in a more interesting and entertaining encounter.

4. **Make the user acquisition enjoyable:** To prevent a high churn rate, recruiting users must be entertaining. It's also crucial to give users all of the data they need to operate your application. By providing a more interesting approach to onboarding your users, you can help them get the most out of your software over time while also having fun and learning.

There are five gamification concepts for applications that you should be aware of:

1. A progress indicator is a smart way to keep users interested and encouraged. You can also use a points system or award your users with in-app badges. For learning software, this may mean keeping track of how much time they spend studying and how well they do on quizzes. Run times, calorie counts, and the amount of exercises performed each week may all be displayed in fitness applications.

2. You can retain users by compensating them for what they do in the application. Incentivize users to execute particular tasks with real benefits. This can enhance transaction length and retention, giving you and your users a win-win situation. The sort of incentives you provide will be determined by the app's structure. If you have a fitness tracker,

for instance, you might partner with relevant manufacturers to provide active users with discounts on sports equipment and healthy meals. This is an excellent way to stimulate people while also expressing gratitude for their brand attachment.

3. Polls may be integrated into any smartphone app to allow users to test their expertise and review relevant data. One of the benefits of integrating quizzes in your smartphone app is that they are very easy to share. Users may wish to share their findings on social media to urge others to download and test your app for free. Users who desire to improve over time might utilize such tests to do so.

4. You may add a competitive nature to your user scoreboards in addition to quiz and point-based schemes that inspire your users. This might be consumer scoreboards or standings that display a user's friends and children's accomplishments, due to the nature of your business. This gives users the chance to climb a scoreboard while also adding a social component to your smartphone app.

5. When users complete particular activities and milestones, you may award them with in-app certificates that appear on their profile. This is a clever way to acknowledge a user's accomplishments and provide them with special prizes for their participation. Badges can also encourage users to pursue more lofty goals. You may take it a step further by providing unique material and tools to customers who have earned particular

certifications. Using smartphone game inspirations to develop your app may also help you maximize your customer acquisition attempts. These components encourage users to return to your app and provide possibilities for them to share it with their friends and family.

As you may have already gathered, there are many advantages and benefits for your brand in implementing gamification in your marketing strategy. Next, we break down the top seven benefits and explain why they're so effective in the digital world.

As users are encouraged to take specific actions with gamification, engagement rates are often higher and better than those achieved in previous campaigns. Commitment can be the first step in a long-term relationship between the customer and the brand.

As mentioned, customers who keep your brand name in their mind for a long time after having a fun experience are a valuable resource to your business.

Data is perhaps one of the most valuable assets for companies today. Combined with complex AI, IoT, and machine learning systems, gigantic databases can provide companies with the tools they need to target the best customers, with the right offer, at the best possible time and place. However, collecting that data isn't always easy and that's where gamification comes in. By offering users the chance to have fun or win a prize or reward, they are likely more willing to give you potential data that you can then use to gain a better understanding of your target audience.

As players engage with the gamified elements your brand provides, they are more likely to respond to your CTA than a traditional banner ad or any other marketing method, in order to win the rewards you have linked to the interactive experience. This will help improve your conversion rates. For example, imagine offering users a 20% discount from a quick interactive quiz on your website. It is likely that the users will take advantage of that discount and proceed to use it to make purchases on your store or e-commerce site.

Consumer behavior can, many times, be more emotional than rational. Often, the same offer or product can be interpreted differently, depending on the context and circumstances of the approach. For example, users may ignore a clickable banner that advertises a 10% discount in the next few hours, but they may feel very excited to be rewarded with the same 10% discount for passing three levels in an interactive game. This is because customers will feel that they have "earned" the discount, that they have "fought" for it, so they will rate it differently than when it is given for no reason.

Gamification marketing can be a fun and easy way to explain the main benefits of your product or service and thereby educate users. For merchants, the ultimate goal of advertising their product or service with ads on websites and apps is to attract and capture new customers. The first step is to capture the attention of users and encourage them to interact with the ad unit. Banner ads and pop-ups are often rejected or ignored by users who are tired of seeing their journey interrupted by unsolicited ads. So, trying to spread your message through a fun and easy to play game can be a good way to reach new users and convert them into customers a few steps later.

Drawbacks to Gamification

Without a doubt, gamification marketing can help you improve your digital presence, increase engagement and interaction with your customers, and collect data that would otherwise be difficult for your company to acquire. However, there are a couple of things you should keep in mind before moving forward with a gamification project for your brand. First of all, making good games requires great creativity. Making basic games, like simple quizzes or tests, is easy, but it's fair to say that users don't get much of this type of experience and are unlikely to proceed to the next step if they are presented with one of these games.

Therefore, your brand should consider getting advice from an experienced creative agency to design and develop fun and proven educational games that will capture the attention of your leads. This process usually takes two things: time and money. Game development usually leads to longer work times than traditional instructional design.

Each step of the design process, from explaining the concept to the project stakeholders, through design and development, to the final test of the game, takes several hours by highly skilled developers, graphic designers, and web designers. For example, games that feature music and a variety of sound effects, photos, videos, or even customized animated elements that enrich the user experience will eventually increase the cost (in terms of time and money) of the project.

Avoiding the Drawbacks

When you incorporate game elements into your business website, you generate interest and subtly encourage visitors to see just how much they can manipulate. Many people find testing the limits of the game to be one of the most engaging parts of it.

Consider an onboarding campaign for a new product line. When customers log in for instructions, they only see a few options. As they investigate each option, others appear. Customers will naturally want to investigate what they have unlocked and see what actions unlock other content.

The downside to keeping content locked behind a progression structure is that some visitors may know exactly where they need to go and don't want to bother clicking through various menus. Consider adding a simple sitemap or toggle so users who aren't interested in playing can get to where they need to go.

However you set it up, just make sure that your game elements don't stop visitors from engaging. Any game element you incorporate should encourage interaction, not force visitors to interact.

While the quality of your content remains paramount, it's vital to deliver content in meaningful ways. People are inherently looking for a logical progression. Psychology is the basis of any content distribution strategy: you have to repeatedly capture the interest of your audience. Most games have some kind of progression.

Typically, it starts in an introductory phase to get players acclimated to the game and its rules. As they progress, they learn more about the parameters of the game. In the end, the game feels natural. But before too long, it can also get boring.

As we seek a logical progression in what we consume, as soon as we focus and identify a new element, our attention begins to diminish. The human mind is extremely quick to notice and focus on a newly introduced visual element. It is vital for marketers to capitalize on the spark of discovery—to encourage moments in which the user suddenly notices or realizes something new and to encourage them to investigate.

A content delivery strategy is based on constantly providing useful and relevant content to recipients. If you don't take the time to understand your audience, your content will fall flat. You can use the elements of the game as a test to understand which types of content work best for your audience. Your customers' profiles should help you devise a great content strategy, and the incorporation of game elements can keep interest alive.

Summary

In this chapter, you learned about the basic concept of gamification, as well as practical examples of gamification in the classroom and how to create gamified-based online apps. The next chapter focuses on new trends, research, and development in HCI.

CHAPTER 8

Human-Computer Interaction Research and Development

This chapter explores new research and developments in the area of human-computer interaction. The fundamental goal of HCI research is to create approaches that will improve people's ability to communicate with machines and make them better and more natural. The use of gadgets for HCI, such as keyboards and mice, reduces the interpretability and naturalness of the interface by creating a significant barrier between the user and the computer. With the rise of pervasive computing, user-computer interaction is no longer restricted to keyboard and mouse interactions. The straight use of hands as input, instead of typical message interfacing through elements user interfaces, is an appealing way to offer more natural human-computer interactions.

Despite the vast market for hand motion user interfaces, conventional vision-based techniques still struggle to construct a reliable hand gesture detection system. As a result, our handwriting recognition system, which can capture both steady and dynamic hand movements, will provide users with a comfortable and intuitive interface to their machines.

With relatively little technology, this system turns the detected motion into activities such as accessing web pages, activating programs, and

© Joseph Thachil George, Meghna Joseph George 2022
J. T. George and M. J. George, *Human-Computer Interaction in Game Development with Python*, https://doi.org/10.1007/978-1-4842-8182-6_8

many others. Another way to make this connection more natural is to employ gaze movements in conjunction with a head-mounted screen, which is a transportable interactive visual equipment that can monitor eye movement as a form of engagement. Because people can easily regulate their eye movements, this approach is very effective and simple to implement. As a result, sight technology may be employed as a human-computer interaction approach. Human-computer interactions are well established for motions and voice input at this time; however, this type of gesture-based human-computer interaction approach is inadequate when both hands are engaged or when language is not available.

As a result, a more straightforward approach to human-computer interaction with head-mounted displays is critical. Additionally, this system performs head-mounted gaze interaction by employing a head-mounted display webcam to identify and monitor the client's needs based on their gaze in real-time at a close range. HCI academic research on gaze motions has exploded in popularity over the years.

Human-Computer Interaction with a Head-Mounted Display

This approach employs eye-tracking, a technology for determining the gaze point of human vision and their amount of motion in relation to head posture. This system utilizes a gaze interaction approach based on a head-mounted display to identify and track human eye movements in real-time at a close distance.

To determine eye movements, the method begins with shooting the eye with the use of a near-eyed camera embedded into the head-mounted display. To directly supply head posture information, the system tailors the range of the head pose distribution. It gathers information based on the range, and this information matches the image acquired by our head-mounted display system. The picture is amplified by a ratio using the pupils as the center.

The pupil dimensions are converted to center coordinates, the pixels are reduced at random, and then Stochastic filtering is performed on the picture. The picture's gaze trajectories are then classified using two modules of deep convolutional neural networks. This network incorporates data from almost 10,000 gaze patterns obtained from a variety of people.

Training from synthesized pictures may not reach the intended results due to the difference in feature concentrations between synthetic and actual images. This network employs a framework pre-trained on the Internet to learn from vast quantities of data and then train the resultant model to bridge the gap between a synthetic picture distribution and a real image dispersion. Using actual data overcomes the problem of distribution of the data and improves system identification while keeping the set of data.

For example, the HTC Vive Oculus Rift (Oculus Quest 2 is the most advanced all-in-one headgear, and Oculus Link gives you access to an incredible library of PC VR games).

Human-Machine Interfaces: Future Development

The human-machine interface constitutes an interface paradigm with artificial systems, in particular the computer, which over time has been defined and developed to overcome the different functional nature of the interaction and communication between machines and human beings. The abstract nature of machines, whatever they are, electronic, mechanical, electromechanical, etc., has given rise over time to the problem of human interaction with the machine and the consequent search for efficient and effective solutions to make such practical interaction. The human-machine interface, in its implementation, is inspired by the nature of human interaction, which is mainly sensory in nature.

Initially, the first interaction devices that made it possible to create human-machine interfaces were of a hardware nature, which with the advent of computers became keyboards, first numeric then alphanumeric, and displays. Thanks to these devices, it has been possible for humans to interact at a high level with machines with a low level of information representation (for example, the binary level of the first computers).

In the first phase of the development of the human-machine interface, the keyboard represented the first form of interface to the machine. The typewriter used the alphanumeric keyboard to allow the users to communicate to the typewriter the alphabetic coding of words in terms of operating the hammers that beat the writing roller. Subsequently, the hardware level of the man-machine interface was integrated by the software level, thanks to the development of information processing technologies made possible by the ever-increasing computational power available in computer-based systems.

The introduction of the mouse made it possible to quickly switch from the command-line interface based on an alphanumeric keyboard and alphanumeric display to the graphical user interface based on the mouse and graphic display. In the first phase of the development of electronics, systems used numeric keypads or electromechanical numeric coding systems (e.g., pulse encoding disks of digits in first-generation telephones), and luminous digit display systems to allow interaction with the user at a very low level.

The Touchscreen Revolution

The evolution of the human machine interface has been implemented over time through hardware and software innovations that have occurred because of the evolution of microelectronic technology.

The introduction of touchscreen displays, first for desktop systems, then for palmtop systems, gave a new innovative impulse to the development of the human-machine interface, giving it a level of naturalness that led to the definition of a new paradigm of man-machine interface, the so-called *natural user interface,* based on computational gesture recognition technologies.

Additional technologies, such as motion-sensing technologies based on Mems accelerometric devices and multi-dimensional sensing platforms (accelerometer and magnetometer), made it possible, especially on mobile devices, to create advanced human-machine interfaces. The natural human-machine interface has begun to materialize with the first hardware and software capable of speech recognition and synthesis and image recognition. These technologies of natural interaction with artificial systems have had development on handheld computing platforms, in particular smartphones, thanks to the considerable computing power these devices are equipped with and that these devices can obtain from the network. The use of the computational resources of the network, namely cloud computing, has allowed the implementation of voice recognition systems such as Apple's Siri. This would be impossible to implement in embedded mode on the smartphone, considering its limited computational possibilities in relation to the complexity of real-time voice recognition.

Direct Communication with the Mind

The evolution of the human-machine interface did not stop at the natural user interface, but was projected into the future, almost as a science fiction form of the brain/machine interface. Recent research carried out in the field of neuroscience has shown that it is possible to interact directly with machines, by using the bioelectrical signals generated by the human brain in its cognitive component (i.e., thinking).

Initiated in the 1970s at the University of California Los Angeles, the first research on the brain computer interface developed methods and technologies of direct interactions with computers produced by neural signals. These were captured with previously invasive methods (implanted electrodes), then semi-invasive methods (contact electrodes). Recently, non-invasive methods (electromagnetic fields, ultrasounds) were used.

The last frontier consists of directly implanting chips in the cerebral cortex and capturing and processing the neural signals generated by communication and thought formation activities in humans. In a recent experiment with a chip implanted in the human brain, surprising results have been obtained in communication between human and machine through thought. The brain did not reject the implant and, after a significant period of time, the chip was integrated into the neural tissue and neurons even grew on the surface of the chip.

Human-machine interface has become very important in computer-based systems, so much so that with the massive development of embedded systems, it has become one of the primary functional components. Developers and manufacturers of microelectronic technologies for embedded systems have paid particular attention to this development, developing components to support it. This was justified above all by the computational complexity of the human-machine interface and by the difficulty of developing application platforms with scarce resources such as embedded systems, as well as by the extremely limited development times typical of these embedded systems.

Gesture Engagement Taken to a New Level

Gestural interaction, as an interactive component of the human-machine interface, has materialized with the introduction of the touch function in second-generation displays. Touch-based gesture recognition has shown all its limitations, especially in terms of versatility and generalization of the gesture, as well as lack of naturalness. The most recent of the devices that incorporate GestIC gesture recognition technology is the MGC3030/3130 Tracking and Gesture Controller.

This controller integrates on a single chip the mixed-signal technology for controlling the variations of an electric field through five electrodes, four of which are for the horizontal coordinates (x, y) and a central one for the vertical coordinate (z). The technology of signal processing for the execution of the pattern recognition functions for the recognition of gestures in 3D. The chip integrates a dedicated DSP and a ROM memory of predefined and preceded patterns as useful gestures for interacting with the system.

Applications of Spatial Cognition Human Contact Research

Human-computer interaction is an important part of human factor science and engineering in smart factories. The natural human interface adapts to the users' thinking processes and can readily absorb erroneous information exchanges, improving user experience and reducing cognitive strain. Analyzing the communication and interactions yields a cognitive-driven human-computer interaction information transmission model. One can examine the process by engaging modes, as well as the system's application status, technological demands, and difficulties, in the present human-computer interaction system.

In order to detect inaccurate information and guide the design and enhancement of human-computer interaction systems, it is critical to recognize the assessment methods in human-computer systems from three tiers of subjective evaluation, biological quantification, and arithmetical method evaluation. Based on the current status of human-computer interaction in exploiting a variety, the inquiry topics, problems, and growth patterns of human connection are described.

Entry, analysis, and output are the three steps of the data transfer process between humans and computers. Among the three phases, the information entry step is the only one in which consumers must actively participate. If the collaborative and interactive mode of information input is easy to learn and use, and if it matches people's cognitive modes, the authenticity of the user interaction is defined, and users have reduced cognitive load throughout the communication.

People have five senses—sight, touch, listening, feeling, and taste. Using input equipment, input data channels may be divided into categories and their correlations, such as vision-camera, app, listening, smell-smell sensors, taste and texture detector, and so on. The information output is the machine system's response to the user's input, and the users may use it to determine if the interaction was successful, precise, and natural.

Knowing and modeling human-machine-environment interaction is a significant topic in natural human-computer interaction. The human-computer interaction data processing system is based on human contact, with the interface design principle serving as a limiting element. It incorporates the human-computer interaction process, user experience, and cognitive information.

According to the user information processing model, the user analyzes information and makes response actions after receiving data stimulation through the information vision technology, the user cognition system, and the user reaction system. The information perception system in the human-computer interaction information processing model stores the stimulus signal in short-term memory and performs judgmental sampling after the output data is viewed by the human through perceiving streams like hearing and sight.

Design requirements for human-computer interaction systems are provided by the user cognitive system. The data supplied, for example, should be categorized and structured in accordance with the relevant connections. The user response system demands that the design reduce the cognitive burden imposed on individuals by the information transmitted, such as minimizing the frequency with which users change mouse and keyboard keys and reducing unnecessary visual motion.

Interaction with the Voice

Language processing technology is required for interaction. Call routing, voice to text, machine manipulation, and other language processing applications are available. At the moment, voice interaction is mostly used at the level of voice listening and speech control systems. Medical records, legal and business records, and general word processing are among the application sectors at the phonological transcription level. Some patients with physiological impairments may benefit from voice interactive input to assist them better enter phrases or other activities.

Physical language is widely accepted as a prevalent form of communication. The aims of gesture interaction may be broken into two categories: increasing user autonomy and initiative, and providing advanced smart services. Prior research has looked at posture as a kind of human-computer interaction.

Interactions Between the Brain and the Computer

Brain-computer interfaces can detect a user's optic nerve impulses and employ algorithm software to turn the feedback signals into actions, i.e. the cognition regulates the user's behavior. Accepting, deciphering, encoding, and response are the steps in the BCI interactive information transmission process. Receiving signals from functioning matching neurons and utilizing computer chips and programming, the particular operation translates the information into machine operations.

Customer work assessments can be used to measure the efficacy of human-computer interaction modes. A significant number of studies have been conducted. Psychological evaluation techniques, physiologic measurement techniques, and quantitative evaluation methods are the three types of usability evaluation approaches for personal communication.

User narrative coherence, learnability, and satisfaction are examples of subjective assessment markers. During the process of calculating the weight of assessment indexes, mathematical approaches and models such as gray theory analysis, clustering algorithms, fuzzy arithmetic, and the analytical hierarchical process are used. Currently, there are multiple physiological assessment methods to assess the usefulness of human-computer interaction mode: eye-gaze tracking and electroencephalography. These two technologies have become the focus and center of study.

According to such studies, it is suggested that in-depth conversations be held on the following topics. Because human behavior is more informal and has ambiguous connotations, computer vision's detection of actions and erroneous information is insufficient, and the effort of rectifying, analyzing, and recovering enormous data at a later time is also high.

The organic engagement mode is now significantly dependent on the success of each sensor. The precision of sensor data fusion is poor. The track inaccuracy and information interaction latency have a significant impact on interaction effectiveness. To increase the efficiency of data recognition process, interface technologies must be upgraded. Information devices will cause a virtual tactile perception to differ from actual tactile perception in the consumer experience.

At the security requirements, the production of human behavior data must be further ensured. Personal privacy problems, for example, must be assessed for security procedures in voice commands.

Human-computer interaction is rapidly progressing to the level of human-computer integration. First and foremost, machines and equipment may organically interact with the world and humans, adapting to a complex diverse working environment and cooperating with one another. Secondly, in the domains of smart factories, medical rehabs, and defensive military security areas, the necessity for natural human-computer interaction is rapidly expanding.

As a result, it is vital to do research on human-computer interaction theory and design approaches that combine the human-computer-environment. Lastly, via multi-disciplinary cross-integration, human-computer interaction needs to produce novel information-gathering development in multi-modal detection of objects, human-computer mutual adaptation and collaboration, swarming smart interaction operating systems, and other areas.

On a technological level, the data drive of human-computer interaction design perceptions is investigated in order to meet the need for big and complicated results of a process in key sectors. It simplifies the design of human-computer integrated robotic arms, addresses natural communication issues such as living body drive, perspective, natural human-computer interaction enhancement, and neural perception and control, and advances the use of composable, decentralized human-computer interaction operating systems.

More natural and efficient interaction strategies have been explored in human-computer interaction research. After years of research, significant progress has been made, with a strong growth tendency. We think that the advancement of new human-computer interaction will result in more fresh ideas being presented to people in a much more natural and effective manner. In recent years, the research community has focused on artificial intelligence and machine learning in the context of computer interface techniques.

HCI is the study of the development, assessment, and use of information and communications technology with the objective of improving user experiences, task performance, and overall quality of life. Artificial intelligence and intelligent augmentation applications are constantly being formed and shaped by HCI. As a result, new and intriguing study subjects are rapidly emerging. These subjects, as well as the challenges they raise, stretch and test our present theoretical underpinnings and research approaches. This necessitates contemplation and debate among IS academics.

This track intends to provide a venue for researchers to explore, create, and disseminate new ideas, techniques, and empirical discoveries relevant to HCI, AI, and/or IA phenomena. We invite articles that address new and developing challenges in these domains and reflect a variety of academic disciplines and techniques, such as behaviors, economics of information systems, microeconomics, design science, and information science.

Research relevant to the track may offer novel theoretical perspectives on HCI, AI, and IA in a variety of situations. These include but are not limited to e-commerce, m-commerce, human labor, institutions, interpersonal contact with advanced devices, human robot interactions, novel connectivity designs for augmented worlds reality innovations, and investigation of HCI issues using neural circuits instruments (e.g., GSR and eye-trackers).

Relevant studies have looked at the impact of AI on corporate strategy creation, implementations in public versus private businesses, the impact of AI on the market, economics, and community, as well as the business advantages and unexpected repercussions of AI.

Summary

Human-computer interaction is the study of how computers are designed and used, particularly communications protocols, in order to find new and better ways to communicate data and activities between humans and machines. Affective computing, which includes automatic emotion identification from physiological signs, video, and sound using a machine learning technique, is one of the core subjects of study. In addition, the use of such technologies to monitor human emotions in actual effect systems, robotics, and testing phases is being investigated. Methods for developing and evaluating assistive and instructional technology for persons with disabilities (e.g., central nervous system interfacing), as well as universal design principles for making applications and systems more accessible to everyone, are another area of study.

In this sector, research is conducted in collaboration with medical centers as well as enterprises that produce data gathering and processing facilities and human-computer interaction interfaces.

Current issues and development in HCI include human-technology symbiosis; human-environment interactions; ethics, privacy, and security; well-being, health, and eudaimonia; accessibility and universal access; learning and creativity; and social organization and democracy. However, new virtual reality technologies will enable so many new and unique interactions that they will fundamentally alter how we build user interfaces and interact with computers. Interfaces will no longer be confined to little screens, but will instead exist in our own three-dimensional environments.

The most prevalent influence of HCI on society has been to make everyday living easier by improving the ease with which computers and other gadgets may be used. Most devices may now be used by people who have never had any instruction.

Artificial intelligence is a field of the design and application of machine learning techniques for a wide range of applications, including information retrieval, data processing, data categorization, and inference engine construction. This includes language learning for extracting data from message sources, intelligent methods for getting data from still pictures and bitstreams, and machine learning. Artificial Intelligence is inspired by human intelligence and empowered by data. This course will teach you how to harness the power of artificial intelligence to make it positive and useful to humans. We'll go through agency and initiative, AI and ethics, bias and transparency, confidence and mistakes, human enhancement and amplifying, trust and interpretability, and programming by example, to name a few subjects. Research in dialogue and voice-controlled systems, automated voice recognition, machine learning, data science, recommendation systems, text categorization, cognitive science, UI customization, and visualization will be used to investigate these subjects.

CHAPTER 9

Recommendations and Concluding Comments

Human-computer interaction (HCI) is an academic subject that focuses on how humans and machines communicate at each and every level. Most of us think of HCI as user experience design. Because of the subject's relevance, this book contains more relevant material to students, scholars, and industry researchers who want to learn more about its real-time applications.

This book examined the fundamental causes of mental, social, and organizational difficulties, in addition to giving information on theory, cognition, design, assessment, and user experiences. Typically, rehabilitation strategies for particular cognitive processes are described. The novel modeling methods available to scientists from a range of fields are also discussed.

Recommendations

HCI became particularly popular as personal computers became more common in companies and households. Gaming units, word processing,

J. T. George and M. J. George, *Human-Computer Interaction in Game Development with Python*, https://doi.org/10.1007/978-1-4842-8182-6_9

and numerical assistance were the origins of this notion. As a result, the demand for tools for the less experienced grew, indicating that it was time to make HCI simpler. As a result, HCI broadened to include areas such as computer science and computer neuroscience.

This branch of research has become an important tool for engaging with computers in order to make them as human-like as feasible. Originally, HCI aimed to improve the usability of personal computers. With the introduction of the Internet and smartphones, computing has shifted away from desktop computers and to mobile phones and smart gadgets. Nowadays, HCI is a large field of research that includes topics like user-centered design, user interfaces, and user experience design.

Broad HCI Assessment Criteria

Interfaces are predicted to become more interwoven into daily life in the future, rather than only on screens, and to be configurable and omnipresent. The end outcome will be a society where technology is experienced via all senses rather than simply through a display. Figure 9-1 shows the basic HCI assessment criteria.

Usability	User Experience
Fewer errors	Aesthetically pleasing
Efficient	Pleasant and fun
Easy to learn	Motivating and engaging
Easy to remember	Reliable
Safe to use	Satisfying

Figure 9-1. *HCI assessment criteria*

This shift has been noticeable in the previous decade, and it is mirrored in the tremendous technical advancements of smartphones and mobile devices, which have resulted in a plethora of new interactions.

HCI is also changing, as seen by touch displays and the use of speech to communicate with gadgets. A tiny portion of the possibilities of this form of interaction include the capacity to plan meetings, scour the web, and manage chores by speech.

Hardware resources such as the mouse or keyboard were used as HCI aids in the past, but they hampered intuition and genuineness of the interaction, which was a hurdle to maximizing the user's computing capability. As a result, in this field, being able to engage with the system as organically as possible is crucial and becoming extremely relevant. The use of fingers as an input device, rather than message interfaces, is an appealing technique.

with voice commands, the innovation is likely to be adopted at a rate of more than 80 percentage points in the next six years. This is due to the fact that it is simple to use, quick, and effective. Touching will likely continue to be the most popular mode of engagement, but speech is gaining momentum, albeit not all options have yet been explored it is a more deep way of communicating with gadgets.

In addition, in the coming years, virtual reality is predicted to rise quickly. In addition to acquiring Oculus, Facebook has rebranded itself Meta. Google has Cardboard and ARCore, while Microsoft has the HoloLens, a virtual reality headset. This means that when more major corporations enter the industry, the amount of money invested will increase, and innovations will begin to appear.

These new interactive virtual devices, like smartphones before them, will revolutionize the way interfaces are built and even how systems are interacted with. Interactions will no longer be on displays, but will instead be embedded in the 3D reality around us. This shift is likely to be incremental, but architects will need to get familiar with new 3D design methodologies as augmented worlds and virtual reality become more prevalent.

Wearable tech is also making rapid progress. For instance, the Apple TV has new features such as the ability to observe another heart rate and the ability to use the electronic crown, exactly like on your phone. These gadgets will become less expensive, more useful, and less reliant on smartphones over the next several years.

Very likely, the wearable industry will change so drastically in the future decades that it will no longer resemble the one we know now, where smartwatches, bracelets, and shoes currently exist. Ultimately, a procedure will be initiated that will allow this technology to be implanted into our bodies to monitor the most critical vital indicators and provide the wearer with a continuous and exact record of their physical abilities. The advantages to human health if it were to become widely implemented would be significant.

Experiments for the creation of interfaces based on hand signals have also begun. Conventional ways, on the other hand, have difficulties in developing a reliable hand gesture detection system.

The goal is to create a hand gesture detection system that can effectively record both static or dynamic motions, resulting in a technology that is easy and natural for people to use. With minimum technology, this system turns the recognized motion into actions such as accessing web pages or activating programs, among many others.

Because this contact is so natural, the gaze would be a perfect user interaction. It would necessitate the usage of a user's face display (head-mounted display), which is a wearable interactive visual gadget that can track eye gaze for engagement. Because humans can readily regulate their eye movements, this technology would be a breakthrough because it is both effective and simple. Eye-tracking technologies are cutting-edge tools for HCI.

The last option is the most straightforward and most successful for HCI with HDM. This system uses a camera to do deep neural network models gaze communication, detecting and tracking gaze direction in real time at close range and analyzing what the users want to communicate. This tendency is being examined and is fast expanding, despite the fact that it appears to be far off.

In a nutshell, HCI involves study into new methods for people to engage with new technology systems, with the goal of developing practical and functional processes that suit the requirements of the consumers who use them.

This style of engagement aims to lessen the amount of physical and mental effort necessary to use modern technology, in such a way that a game's productivity is directly influenced by its simplicity of use. As a result, HCI strives for user ease while still attempting to be as economical as feasible.

The emotional side of a system relates to the people who utilize it. In the meantime, a computer is any electrical device or device that takes, processes, and transmits data using software or hardware coding. Interaction is the term used to describe the relationship between the two ideas. Due to advances in technology, like voice search and eye-tracking, major advancements in this field of study are predicted in the coming years, with the goal of improving general user interfaces and users' quality of life.

Information and Communication Technology (ICT) Development

Users and engineers in the early years of computer engineering devoted far less attention to creating equipment/software systems that were useable and easy to navigate. However, requests from an increasing proportion of consumers for simple-to-use technologies finally drew the attention of academics.

Accessibility is defined by the World Organization for Standardization as the capacity of a product to be used by specific users to achieve specific goals with speed, efficiency, and pleasure in a specific context of usage. As a result, accessibility refers to a collection of characteristics that are mostly connected to computer networks, such as efficiency, security, and usefulness.

Other key idea connected with usability in the early 1990s is user experience. It's primarily concerned with aspects of the user's experience, such as pleasure, enjoyment, positive attachments, visual value, and so on. In several study fields, the idea of user experience has been expanded and better defined. The User Experience Hexagon, for example, is frequently used by web interface designers to determine priorities throughout the design phase. The honeycomb's eight hexagonal shapes symbolize factors that must be meticulously balanced to ensure that an interface is helpful, useable, desired, obtainable, approachable, believable, and worthwhile to users.

A further crucial aspect of HCI is comprehending human mental representations. Consumers acquire and maintain information and skills in a variety of methods, which are typically impacted by their age, as well as their cultural and social backgrounds. HCI research aims to close the gap among users and new technology.

New Trends

For so many years, people have used the keypad paradigm to send orders to "computers." We use a keypad to dial digits on the telephone, interact with a TV, pick a wide range of features on a car dashboard, and many more activities that involve key-based engagement paradigms. In most circumstances, the computer's output to the user is shown on a screen or other video display.

Numerous low-cost sensors have started to change how humans engage with technology. Touching and touchscreens screens have accelerated the transition from cell phones to smartphones, and gestures are now the primary mode of engagement on personal devices. Simultaneously, voice recognition algorithms and the improved computing capability of CPUs enable users to offer inputs even when they are unable to do motions.

Devices like the Microsoft Kinect are taking us one step closer to fully natural interfaces in which the body serves as the control. The gadget allows users to give orders to the computer through gestures and body positions, while embedded circuitry processes raw data from a camera module in real time, resulting in a design of a skeletal system. The technology can recognize stances and gestures by detecting the location and direction of bones, which may then be transferred to machine instructions.

Devices that track a government's hands have also been proposed by the researchers. The Magic Leap, for example, can monitor both hands of a user actively by recognizing the locations of fingertips and the palms, then it calculates pinkie fingers using a kinematic solution. In place of typical touch displays for controlling infotainment services, some automakers are already offering a hand-tracking based alternative engagement modality. Similarly, some smart TVs have replaced the standard TV remote with a series of gestures that allow viewers to select their selections.

The possibilities outlined previously, which were seen in science fiction movies only a few years ago, are now a reality in HCI. New and more exciting situations, on the other hand, look to be on the horizon, with brain connections ready to reverse the interaction between people and robots, for example. Future technological breakthroughs, which aim to turn interface devices into wearable and composable things, will be critical to the success of this new interaction paradigm. This change is seen in interfaces based on augmented reality technology. Many apps for travel, leisure, housekeeping, commerce, and social networking are now accessible for personal devices, but new wearable sensors may transform our routines in the near future.

New types of HCI will have a huge impact on our lives. This new communication paradigm has the potential to improve the quality of life for those who are unable to use contemporary interfaces due to physical limitations. New challenges, such as privacy, security, and ethics, will emerge, possibly impeding the adoption of new hardware and software products built on these wearable technologies. Even though some scholars have looked at the links between interface design and legal and privacy concerns, national law is fragmented and unprepared to deal with current and future improvements in HCI.

Promising HCI Technologies

Hundreds of innovations are being evaluated at HCI right now that will transform how humans interface with machines in the future. We'll merely name the first ones that spring to mind for the purpose of brevity. Large multi-touch displays, for example, turn a table or a wall into an interactive object on which our hands glide to engage with more natural motions than those forced on us by keyboards and mice. Or there are the androids (anthropomorphic robots with human characteristics that have achieved an astonishing level of realism), who will make the user-machine connection easier, owing to their forms and communication techniques, which are more human-like than ever before.

It's to the point that one wonders if the interaction between humans and humanoids would go so far as to address the emotional or affective level as well. Alternatively, there may be interfaces that detect the user's encephalogram in order to receive orders based on what the user thinks; or those that assess physiological parameters in order to determine what emotional state the user is in and modify communication techniques and functionalities based on that emotional state.

HCI encompasses all aspects of interactive system design, assessment, and development, as well as the study of all surrounding phenomena. On this topic, the researchers have been conducting a wide variety of study for several years with the goal of enhancing the user experience with current interactive systems that now influence several aspects of an individual's life, such as health, work, leisure time, mobility, and so on. All of the lines of study carried out at the laboratory are fed by a suitable balance of creativity, curiosity in future technologies, and expertise in the field of usability engineering. These have piqued my curiosity in recent years:

- User experience (UI design and collaborative design, as well as their applicability in software engineering processes)

- Communication in multiple modes

- Healthcare on the go

- User acceptance testing

- Developing regions and ICT

- Coupling of human-geographic information management

- Geographical visualization

- Geographic information system visible queries interfaces

- Design methodologies for usable and accessible software applications

- Quality models and website quality assessment techniques

- End-user development

- Natural interaction with intelligent systems

- User interfaces for decision support systems and planning systems

- Interfaces to complex physical systems (plants, control systems, etc.)

- Interaction customization techniques

- Innovative models of interaction with cooperative robots

Important Considerations for Building a User-Friendly Interface

Your focus should be on the customers and the activities they will complete at the outset of the any design project, as well as who those users will be. Is it necessary for the user to have some level of competence in a certain field? When would that particular duty be completed? Is there any use of non-standard designs and/or iconography in the interface?

These are the kinds of questions you need to address before you start working on these interfaces. After that task is done and you have a clear understanding of what you want to achieve with your UI, you can begin developing a model and testing it with actual users. You should never begin construction without first testing with real users, as they will be the ones who will use the interfaces, and you don't want to waste time developing something that will be useless.

You will be able to determine what is functioning and alter what is not in the prototypes after evaluating customer feedback. You can truly start developing the interfaces when you obtain what you believe is a decent outcome with the prototype. It's critical to remember that you should continue to use the same immersive model for implementing, testing, and, if necessary, modifying the interfaces. The following are some suggestions for optimal actions:

- *Keep your interaction components legible.* If the text or items being presented aren't visible, they can't be used properly.

- *It's crucial to have redundant information.* If a message is provided several times, it's more likely to be comprehended correctly. The term "duplication" doesn't really mean "repeating." Colors and placement are contradictory in a traffic signal, which is an excellent illustration of duplication.

- *Employ distinguishing components to avoid being confused by similarities.* Signals that appear to be the same will very certainly be mixed up. Identical aspects should be deleted, if possible, while distinctive features should be emphasized.

- *Use many assets to allow users to absorb input from a range of sources more quickly.* Instead of showing all visual or aural data, for instance, vision and hearing information might be displayed concurrently.

- *Replace memories with visual data.* A user shouldn't have to rely on cognitive function or long-term memory to remember crucial information. A menu, checklist, or other display can help the users by reducing the amount of time they spend using their memories.

- *Do not innovate.* If new interfaces are created properly, old patterns from prior interactions will simply transfer to facilitate the generation of sensory ones. This reality must be accepted, and the design must adhere to the norms that have previously been established in comparable interactions.

Final Thoughts on Game Design and HCI

Although the game industry has made considerable advances in human-computer interaction in recent times, the techniques and quantity of information transmission between gamers and computers remain limited, thereby limiting game interactivity and fun. This book presents and discusses the principles of HCI in game design—simple, intuitive, pleasant, and consistent.

As a significant aspect and essential component of the game, connection is a major influence in determining the game's quality. The notion of "clear, intuitive, pleasant, and consistent" should be mirrored in every part of the game's development, according to Don Norman's philosophy of HCI. When these ideas are applied flexibly to the design of an interactive experience, it not only creates effective lines of communication among gamers and computers, but it also increases the game's enjoyment value. Nevertheless, you must keep in mind that these ideas are abstractions. The major features and the follow-up research are explicit instructions on how to practice these game designs.

In the gaming industry, the research topic aims to be a broad team that demonstrates the research, theory, apps, practice, and verification of HCI toward changing behavior. New scientific methods, including findings from tests and real-world applications, are especially encouraged in this area from these viewpoints. Prospective research topics in the game industry include:

- Critical games using HCI

- Gamification settings

- Non-invasive brain games, such as tournament education, match evaluations, and games in universal health care

- Games that use virtual reality worlds

- Game co-development and co-design

- Machine learning cognition in video games

- In-game comments and stats in real time

- Customized and adaptable services

- Supportive and transportable services

- A mechanism for behavioral modification in HCI-SGs

- Sensor systems computation for HCI-SGs

- Important games for bettering one's standard of living

- Important games for recovery at home or at a hospital

- Instructional sports

- Designing SGs with morals in mind

Summary

The possibilities for HCI are limitless. Advances toward useable and natural human-machine interfaces can bring enormous benefits and profoundly alter daily life.

In the past, the HCI group, which includes both professional groups and people, had only sporadic interactions with policymakers. There is a huge opportunity to leverage the HCI group's efforts and knowledge to interact more with policy areas and inform policymakers. Many of the subjects of interest to the HCI community are today being decided in public policy groups in ways that were not the case two decades ago. Within the HCI group, there is a small, core group of people who are engaged in public policy. Now is the moment to step up efforts to engage more actively with the many public policy groups all across the globe.

Everything will undoubtedly alter dramatically, but the good news is that these significant changes will not occur immediately. That isn't to say that designers should relax on their laurels! Keep up with emerging design trends in these fields and don't be hesitant to start experimenting with new computer systems and design patterns. It's the most effective technique to prepare yourself for the new world to follow.

You learned about HCI tools and methodologies in the first two chapters, which you can utilize to create interactive games. Those approaches, including the eye-tracking methodology, have lately been investigated by researchers and new successful applications have been applied. Building real-time applications by employing these technologies was demonstrated in Chapters 3 to 6. The book's conclusion is provided in Chapters 7 and 8, which discussed gamification in the industry.

Index

W, X, Y, Z

Printed in the United States
by Baker & Taylor Publisher Services